THE PASSENGER

THE PASSENGER

HOW A TRAVEL WRITER LEARNED
TO LOVE CRUISES & OTHER LIES
FROM A SINKING SHIP

Chaney Kwak

GODINE | BOSTON | 2021

Published in 2021 by
Godine, Publisher
Boston, Massachusetts

The author is grateful to the editors of the following
magazines, where portions of this book appeared in
slightly different forms: *Hemispheres, StoryQuarterly.*

LIBRARY OF CONGRESS CATALOGING-IN-PUBLICATION DATA
Names: Kwak, Chaney, 1979- author.
Title: The passenger : how a travel writer learned to love
  cruises & other lies from a sinking ship / Chaney Kwak.
Description: Boston : Godine, 2021.
Identifiers: LCCN 2020054421 (print) | LCCN
  2020054422 (ebook)
ISBN 9781567926972 (hardback)
ISBN 9781567926989 (ebook)
Subjects: LCSH: Viking Sky (Ship) | Shipwrecks–Norway. |
  Kwak, Chaney, 1979–Travel.
Classification: LCC G530.V535 K93 2021 (print) | LCC
  G530.V535 (ebook) | DDC 910.9163/24–dc23
LC record available at https://lccn.loc.gov/2020054421
LC ebook record available at https://lccn.loc.
  gov/2020054422

First Printing, 2021
Printed in the United States of America

For my parents, survivors

AUTHOR'S NOTE

This book recounts my firsthand experience as a passenger aboard the Viking Sky *when the ship suffered a complete engine failure on March 23, 2019, and began drifting toward the shore. Sections written in the third-person point of view are based on video footage as well as interviews I conducted with rescue workers, who read the transcripts of their interviews and suggested corrections as necessary. All sources used in the writing of this book—such as interviews, video footage, investigative reports, and newspaper articles—are listed at the end of the book. Although the names of public figures are accurate, in order to protect the privacy of the members of crew, I have altered their names. There are no composite characters.*

1:58 p.m.

As the cruise ship almost tips over, the horizon that once bisected my lovely balcony door rises like a theater curtain and disappears. Now the sea is the stage. I tumble off my bed onto the floor and roll like a stuntman.

For now the ship has yet to fully flop, though it feels like we're getting pretty close. Lucky us, the modern ocean liner is an engineering marvel equipped with technologies ensuring that it always stays upright. We've been rolling dangerously during a nasty storm but recover and list upright after each pounding wave threatens to capsize us.

People's screams pierce my cabin walls, louder at times than the clang of broken kitchen equipment above. Water glasses fling themselves against my cabin door as if possessed.

"Code Echo! Code Echo! Code Echo!" a man's voice crackles over the PA system.

Then, after a loud bang, all is quiet. The heating vent sighs one last time and stops hissing. The television screen goes blank.

The ship leans, as if in slo-mo. It should snap back and right itself.

I wait. And wait.

But we keep falling.

Earlier in the morning

Before panic united us, boredom did.

We had been sailing up and down the coast of Norway for more than a week, alternating between placid fjords and the open sea. Each day, the ship dropped anchor at a new port and unleashed all 915 passengers onto snow-packed streets and into shops brimming with handknit sweaters. We rode in sleighs pulled by steaming reindeers, squinted our eyes at 7,000-year-old rock carvings, and bathed in sunlight filtered through the stained glass of a titanium cathedral. And we witnessed the northern lights—the reason many of us came on this cruise.

Once accustomed to the dopamine hit that a new locale brings each day, your brain begins to take the novelty for granted. You develop a sudden aversion to the mundane. I did, anyway. Yesterday, the captain blamed high winds and rough waves for the cancellation of a scheduled port-call at Bodø, just above the Arctic Circle. Today was yet another stormy day without docking, which meant we were left to amuse ourselves on this floating, 465-cabin complex. We were bored to death.

The cruise's entertainment listing had no shortage of options—or alliterations, for that matter. Would I enjoy the "calming classical compositions" brought to life by the resident cellist? Or immerse myself in the existential angst of *Munch Moments*, a digital art exhibit memorializing the "magic of this master," Edvard Munch?

To be honest, as I read that entertainment brochure, I was a little jealous of whoever wrote it. I was on the cruise to write a feature for a travel magazine, and though that may sound enviable, I was pretty certain the brochure writer had been paid a lot more than I would earn for my article. I've grown jaded beyond repair after a decade of carouselling in the freelance trade. It no longer thrilled me to see my name in publications I'd revered. I was constantly chasing assignments, then running after the editors all over again to get paid. I used to put up with all that hassle for the sheer joy of seeing the world. These days, assignments felt less like travel and more like procrastination before I'd start my real grown-up life.

Desperate for stimulation, I turned up for the morning quiz hour at the Explorers Lounge, the ship's glass-ensconced living room at the bow on Deck 11. I sank into a chaise with a slice of Success Cake, which, Google told me, is a Norwegian specialty of almond meringue and egg cream. Teaming up with a group of snow-haired passengers who were three, maybe four decades older, I tried to answer questions about minor Henry VIII wives and milestone World War battles. Since Viking Ocean Cruises advertises heavily on PBS, it attracts a certain demographic, the type of people who actually want to geek out on Baroque palaces and the Marshall Plan in their free time. Without Google, I was an empty vessel. Needless to say, I got my ass handed to me. So much for that Success Cake.

Earlier that morning, the dark sea and bruise-colored clouds had sandwiched a sliver of blue sky. By the time the quiz finished, the blue ribbon had disappeared and near-horizontal rain lashed at us. The ship pitched violently, rising and bouncing as we penetrated deeper into the storm. Still, from all the way up here on Deck 11, hundreds of feet above the sea, even the largest waves seemed like ripples in a bathtub.

"Wait till my grandkids see this," said one of my quiz teammates, thrusting her phone at me to film her against the window.

We were about to enter Hustadvika, the eleven-mile stretch of coastline—shorter than the length of Manhattan—between the towns of Kristiansand and Molde. Intricate fjords burst into a confetti of rocks here, but unlike other parts of the Norwegian coast, there are no islands to slow down the waves. The untamed North Atlantic douses the shallow reefs hard and makes this well-traveled shipping channel tricky to navigate. Shipwrecks lie underwater, such as that of a 300-year-old Dutch merchant vessel once loaded with yellow bricks. Even experienced fishermen run aground here. *The Admiralty Sailing Directions*—the authoritative, seventy-five-volume navigation reference for merchant mariners—warns seafarers of this "notoriously dangerous" region, especially when "strong winds from SW to NW raise a large steep swell with hollow breaking seas" . . . like today. Hustadvika is no place to be when a storm is brewing.

By noon, heavy planters began sliding around the Explorers Lounge like Ouija pieces. A ceiling panel dropped on a passenger. The art of building a cruise ship involves furnishing it with objects meant to remain immovable in the roughest seas. Now, pieces that were once bolted down were gliding about like ghosts.

The ship was all funhouse corridors, shifting and turning. Workers fought to tame the chlorinated geyser that had once been the indoor pool.

As I half-crawled toward my cabin, the ship rolled so hard I had to lie flat against the hallway wall as it threatened to become the hallway floor. A young Chinese waitress, usually chirpy as she poured morning coffee, dropped her tray to grip the railing, wide eyes staring at nothing.

"Have you seen anything like this?" I asked.

She shook her head and clenched her jaw. What was her story? The only child of a middle-class couple who could afford English lessons, setting out after college from her obscure Chinese city of ten million determined to see the world on an adventure of a lifetime? Of course, I had no idea.

And what did she see in me? A suspicious man—most solo male travelers over twenty-five can seem shady—who's been turning up at each meal by himself, rarely talking with fellow passengers who were twice his age. Maybe a divorcé, maybe a son accompanying elderly parents, maybe just a lonely cruise geek?

Well, here we were, both of us at once familiar and unknown, sharing something neither of us had signed up for. As the ship righted itself, we nodded and slid past each other.

Stepping into the shaken snow globe of a dining room, I dodged the salmon fillets and buttery buns flying around. Busboys hugged dirty plates and champagne flutes, trying not to face-plant between the outraged passengers gripping their banquettes. Every few minutes, another wave flipped more beverage carts.

I stepped around the debris and asked the woman manning the ice-cream stand for two scoops—"Chocolate and stracciatella, thanks." She looked at me, incredulous and probably a little disgusted. She still obliged.

During the past month I'd spent aboard all-inclusive cruises, I'd turned into a bottomless pit, trying to fill a growing hollowness by raiding late-night poolside buffets and terrorizing night-shift staff with my jet-lagged room-service orders. So frequent and erratic were my requests that once a kind night-shift cook wrote out "Feel better soon, Chaney" in chocolate syrup on a plate of fruit I had ordered with chicken soup at midnight. No, I didn't feel better.

The beast, seasick or not, had to be fed.

There's a travel industry adage that cruises are for "the over feds, the newly weds, and the nearly deads." I certainly fit into the first category now; it seemed I was about to qualify for the last.

Am I having fun all alone on a cruise, the playground of couples and families? In fact, would it shock you to hear that I've willingly gone on not one but *two* cruises this month, back-to-back?

Three weeks ago, I'd boarded a luxury Italian cruiser from Bali. (And if that sentence makes you want to punch me in the face, I'm right there with you.) I had a butler with the most erect posture unpack my cheap clothes into hard mahogany drawers before wiping down my battered carry-on. I took Balinese-cooking classes, got kneaded by masseuses like a lump of dough, and drank bottles of wine that cost more than my weekly grocery budget. I donned a bow tie and sashayed across the deck under the stars. The ship glided across the South China Sea, which I later described in a magazine article as—forgive me!—"silky." Then I disembarked and flew from Manila over to Bergen, Norway, to do it all over again in the opposite hemisphere.

I know, I know, being a travel writer sounds glamorous on paper. And yes, I have come across plenty of folks who could afford to think of themselves as glamorous long before they ever sold a single piece of writing—a tribe that knows how to swill Veuve Clicquot before noon and not feel even a tiny bit buzzed or guilty. I, on the other hand, snuck into this trade by reviewing hostels and writing penny-pinching advice while attending graduate school in Berlin on a German government scholarship.

I've approached every cruise I've taken like Margaret Mead visiting Papua New Guinea: the most foreign of environments that grows somehow more alien each time I inhabit it. That may be why I kept getting similar assignments from editors without trying: akin to sending a puzzled pacifist to interview Jean-Claude Van Damme while he punches Steven Seagal to pulp. That Bali cruise? The editor in chief of a top travel glossy had emailed me out of the blue. The Norway cruise? I'd been summoned by the head of a can't-buy-it-so-you-need-to-be-in-the-know monthly found only in the libraries of country clubs.

Or maybe it was all just a joke born not out of intention, but from the very unfairness that drives the world of freelance writers: I happened to be available. I knew better than to decline the assignments tossed into my lap.

No. Wait. This is disingenuous. Work wasn't the only reason that sent me on month long trips; if I wanted to make money, and lots more of it, I could have stayed in San Francisco, where I live, and worked for one of the social-media services that everyone hates but uses hourly. Something else was keeping me away from the one-bedroom apartment I shared with Hannes, my partner of sixteen years.

One week ago, on my first night on the Norway cruise, I startled awake sometime between midnight and dawn to see a chartreuse wave shimmer across the television screen. Jet lag had fogged my brain, and it took me a few seconds to realize I had fallen asleep watching the live camera feed from the bridge, the ship's control room. I stared at the screen.

The northern lights!

That's the reason I was here. I'd been hired to rhapsodize about crystalline fjords, pristine mountains, and the tastefully decorated ship, whose interior is so Nordic that even all the wood fixtures are blond. But the protagonist of the article was to be the aurora borealis, the notoriously fickle light show that takes place in the earth's northernmost extremes. Without seeing it, I'd have no story. And without a story, my article would sputter out and fetch me nothing more than the dreadful consolation prize for freelancers: a kill fee of a couple of hundred dollars.

I sprang out of bed and ran to the top deck. Blades of Arctic air slashed my face. I spun around and around, looking. Icy mountains carved geometric outlines into the night sky, bright with the moon and stars. But no northern lights anywhere.

Defeated, I trudged through the maze of hallways. A cruise ship is a city, a pulsing entity with its own rhythm and character. An invisible network of wires and pipes props up a thriving economy. And like any other city, it can be a very lonely place, especially at night when it shines harshly for the workers and insomniacs who wander as if stuck in the time zone of their faraway homelands. And there's no loneliness greater than the kind you feel when you're surrounded by hundreds, thousands of others.

Back in my cabin, I called the front desk.

"No, no northern lights tonight. The infrared makes everything look green," said a chatty receptionist with a Slavic accent. "What you see is not real."

According to the Norwegian Rescue Services, Captain Bengt-Owe Gustafsson, of the *Viking Sky,* issued Mayday at two in the afternoon local time on March 23, 2019, after all four of the engines stalled and the ship began drifting swiftly toward land. The electricity had gone out.

Three years ago, the cruise ship took to the water for the first time. The *Viking Sky* was a baby in every sense of the word, for it was, at about a fifth the size of the largest cruise ship in service, nimble and about ten percent lighter than the *Titanic*. We should have had little trouble navigating the eleven-mile stretch of Hustadvika.

Our ship was on a tight schedule to unload passengers in London and pick up a whole new batch. Cruises are conveyor belts of leisure, always turning. Sure, they can miss a port here or swap an excursion there, but the departure and arrival dates are immutable, for one day's delay can mean hundreds of air tickets to change, hotel rooms to book, and dissatisfied customers to placate. Take it from a travel writer who caters to readers several income brackets above his: Hell has no fury like a First World traveler slightly inconvenienced.

So, with so much on the line, the *Viking Sky* rushed into a nasty storm while the sixty-foot waves and eighty-seven-mile-per-hour winds had canceled all regional ferries, helmed by the saltiest of salt dogs of Scandinavia.

Now, without power, we are at the mercy of a sea that alternates between quick upsurges and muscular undertows. I'm not a poet, so I can't describe this sensation in a gripping yet surprisingly beautiful way. All I can say is that I want to puke my guts out.

In my cabin, the angry sea fills the view out the glass balcony door. We are falling, falling, falling. Below, the shadowy water swirls in a relentless froth, ready to swallow us whole. And just as I'm about to close my eyes and brace myself for the ship to flop, ear-piercing alarms ring through the ship.

A backup generator must have kicked in, and with it whatever device on the ship keeps us upright. Or maybe it was just the dumb luck of a tide gushing from the shore. Slowly, the ship begins rising upright.

The PA system sizzles back to life.

"This is not a drill," the man on the speaker says. "Report to your muster station. Now!"

I get buck naked.

It's a funny thing, the survival instinct. I've heard of "fight or flight," never "strip or skip." My body switches into automatic mode. I set about disrobing, then re-dressing in what I suspect are the warmest and most water resistant of my layers: woolen thermal underwear, a quick-drying synthetic shirt, a lamb's-wool sweater, snow pants, waterproof boots. Then, taking one last look around the cabin, I leave behind my money and camera, but stuff my passport down my crotch. We have drifted so close to Norway's shore that I can almost make out the jagged outline of each boulder. At this rate, the reefs will shred this ocean liner into scrap metal and the currents will scatter all its contents. Wherever I wash ashore, I want my parents to at least know it's me.

2:36 p.m.

haven't gotten very far since I armored up in my passport codpiece.

I am trying to make my way downstairs to the second floor where the two evacuation points are. The idea is that passengers will congregate, then go into lifeboats in clusters. But most passengers are seniors unaccustomed to walking down seven flights of stairs. At each landing, more passengers from that floor bottleneck. Escaping a cruise, it turns out, involves a great deal of standing.

Inside the windowless staircase, I don't feel seasick anymore. I don't feel much of anything, really. Instead, I simply watch as if dozing off while a TV set streams for hours. It takes me minutes to recognize the man directing traffic on one of the floors: the cellist who, under normal circumstances, would be playing Vivaldi in a black suit to a tea-sipping audience of ladies in sensible sweaters and their husbands, who manspread as if they're still steering golf carts. Funny how the outside world's changed at a head-spinning pace, but cruises seem to have retained the social code of an earlier century; the evacuating men deferentially extend their arms to their wives.

The cellist looks like an exhausted carny counting riders for the next bumper car round, his face betraying no emotion. Seeing vaguely familiar people out of their work attire is a jarring experience. Without his comically towering hat, the smiling sous-chef at the poolside buffet turns out to be just a pimply teenager; in sweatpants whose backside is embroidered with JUICY in rhinestones, the bleary-eyed housekeeper looks even smaller than she did before.

"We're fine," says one crew member on the next landing. "We are all going to be fine as long as nobody panics."

"Have you worked on a ship where somebody *did* panic?" I ask him in stage whisper, morbid curiosity piqued.

The man nods gravely, like a veteran recalling a gruesome tour of duty.

"I used to work on a cruise in the Caribbean," he says.

My mind goes into overdrive, conjuring images of buff frat boys from *The Grind*, the 1990s MTV after-school pool-party special, trampling one another's glistening pecs and washboard stomachs. I can also see spray-tanned *Real Housewives* aspirants jumping overboard with glasses of pinot gris still in hand, throwing back one last swig on their way down.

I start taking inventory of everything I see, imagining how my article would open now. The old lead I wrote (something about the northern lights—who cares now?) is out the window. Then I feel hopelessly gross for wanting to write about this moment, as I'm doing now.

When we finally reach the hallway outside the main dining hall, named, quite literally, The Restaurant, the crew has us sit down on the carpeted floor and pass around life vests that smell like dealership cars. They must never have been used except for the half-hour mandatory safety drills. A week before, I attended such a briefing with a drink in hand. Now, sitting cross-legged on the tilting floor, I can recall nothing I was supposed to remember.

I look around and nobody meets my eyes. I'm surprised to see so many new faces. These people and I have been cohabitating in this floating city for more than a week now.

A voice on the speaker, which by now I have come to associate with a semi-omniscient and wholly unhelpful deity, returns. We shush one another.

"Ladies and gentlemen, this is your captain speaking. We now have one of the four engines running, and I will be updating you regularly."

If he meant to reassure us, the intent is lost, at least on me: Until that moment, I had no idea *none* of the engines was working.

A woman nearby, the closest to my age, sniffles and wipes her eyes.

"She's thinking of her little boys," a man who must be her father says to nobody in particular, apologetic. I think about my friends' toddlers, who I'm pretty sure wouldn't remember me. I don't know why I'm being schmaltzy. My friend Faith's newborn daughter, who I might never meet, comes to mind, and I can't believe I'm thinking of this tiny human being I've seen only on a phone screen.

Then I realize I'm trying to put off thinking about the little people who matter the most: my own nieces and nephew.

In a flood of memories, I see all the spinning amusement park teacups and backyard treasure hunts; I remember the diapers I've changed, words I've taught them, and beds we've jumped on. The tear ducts burst open, and I know holding back would only make me hiccup and ugly-cry, so I bury my head between my knees and let out the tears. I could afford to be cavalier about my own safety until now. I even thought up inane jokes about trashy reality shows. The faint possibility that I might disappear from this world didn't exactly devastate me, but now I am overwhelmed remembering all the lives that interlock to carve out my little speck in the world. I finally understand what's at stake.

The door opens into The Restaurant. Like a funeral procession after a bleak memorial service, we shuffle inside. The wine fridge has emptied itself, scattering a field of blood-colored glass shards. We tread over them, the carpet crunching and squishing under our weight, and plant our butts on whatever dry surfaces we can find.

"I. Am. Not. Happy!" says the woman across from me, pouting.

Her husband squeezes her shoulder to comfort her, but she weasels out of his touch, yanking the hand of a crew member who's trying in vain to tidy up.

"Excuse me, excuse me! What will happen with our luggage?" she asks, using the same tone she probably uses to ask for the manager. Her husband says nothing; his is the face of a spouse who hasn't gotten in a word in at least forty years.

Waves douse the portholes, which are usually way

above sea level. From high above, our ship must look like a white flag of surrender, helplessly billowing at an unsympathetic sea that escalates its savage attack. In the last century, we humans have tricked ourselves into believing that we have the upper hand over nature. We've been wrong.

There's a thunderous clap, followed by a crescendo of shrieks. My eyes follow a couple of passengers in bright orange vests jumping out of their seats. Behind them, a crew member lunges while flailing helplessly. A woman flops onto her stomach and gets dragged across the floor as if lassoed. A few passengers get lodged between the legs of the massive dining table. It takes my brain a few seconds to connect the sight with a logical explanation: A swell has hit the ship so high and hard that water has broken through. The sea is gushing in.

Imagine weathering this storm outside the temperature-controlled comfort of the interiors. Imagine standing on the ship's deck, the rain and the ocean lashing across it. Imagine the cold. Imagine the terror.

Above the calamity in The Restaurant, a group of seamen are preparing the lifeboats. There's no room for error. Each evacuation vessel carries 150 people. They can't spend more than a few seconds pushing each passenger into the tender; then the vessels must move away quickly from this dozen-deck liability.

"*Punas, punas!*" shouts one man—"Wipe, wipe" in Tagalog.

"*Calma, calma!*"—"Calm, calm!"

In the grainy cell phone video, posted later on the internet, no face is visible for more than a split second. There are just hands, working at a superhuman pace, unspooling ropes, pulling at the davits.

Then, a white wave roars above the life rafts and erases those bodies.

"*Pasok, pasok, pasok!*" shouts a panicked voice. "Go inside, inside, inside!"

This is where the footage ends.

~

Lifeboats save lives; sometimes, though, they kill. When the RMS *Lusitania* was torpedoed by German submarines in 1915, the ship was a mere eleven miles south of Old Head of Kinsale, a rocky outcrop at the southern tip of County Cork, Ireland. Ten minutes after the attack, the ocean liner was still intact, listing fifteen degrees to starboard. The captain ordered the ship to be abandoned. There were forty-eight lifeboats, each with a capacity of 150: room for more than 7,000 passengers on a ship carrying fewer than 2,000.

In the ensuing chaos, many of the rafts turned upside down as they were lowered, dumping the passengers into the sea. Some overturned when they hit the water, and others tipped when panicked passengers tried to jump in mid air. In the end, the lifeboats carried just 761 people to safety—and 1,198 lives were lost.

Biologically speaking, humans have no business setting out to sea. We have no fins, and saltwater makes our innards burst like fireworks. Maybe that's why ship and airplane disasters grip our attention: They show humans daring into territories where we don't belong—and failing spectacularly.

Then again, maybe it's just the sheer scale of such casualties that captivates us.

We all know about the RMS *Titanic*, considered unsinkable until, well, it sank in 1912. The unfortunate encounter with an iceberg resulted in more than 1,500 deaths and, subsequently, a dozen films, documentaries, and even an animated series—the heart will go on, sure, and so will the books and movies about this famous disaster.

Then there's the HMS *Barham*, which sank off the Egyptian coast in 1941 after being torpedoed by the German submarine U-331. After capsizing, the British battleship's main magazine exploded and killed 862 crewmen. From an adjacent battleship, cameraman John Turner filmed the scene in black-and-white newsreel, capturing the gruesome scene of sailors being flung into the air alongside bits and pieces of the ship in a pall of smoke. The footage keeps going after the explosion. Unflinching, Turner kept filming for prosperity—so that it might inspire moviegoers to enlist, perhaps. Today, history buffs and calamity fetishists watch the footage over and over on You-Tube—five million views and counting! More than 18,000 "likes"! "Up next," YouTube suggests once the clip is over, is a fan video of the same footage, only in slow motion.

Drivers rubberneck at car wrecks. When disasters of greater magnitude happen, the whole world turns to watch. We seem unable to help ourselves. We gawk at catastrophes.

So, what do I do when I'm inside a disaster in the making? Do I hold up a mirror, fascinated? Or do I make fists of white knuckles? Take notes?

3:03 p.m.

I have no choice but to watch helplessly as the frigid saltwater sloshes around The Restaurant and laps about our ankles; not a damn thing I can do. The passengers remain calm and stoic. Oh, Viking Cruises and its commercials on PBS! How fortunate is it that I'm outnumbered by these *Downton Abbey* watchers? These are the kind of people who will sit patiently through pledge drives. So we stay in place, dazed and privately panicking, but politely not trampling one another.

"Kindly put your hand on the shoulder of the person in front of you," someone shouts, her voice clipped and British. "Come on! Well done! Crocodile walk, everyone. Crocodile walk."

I've never heard of The Crocodile, but I'm pretty sure it's not conga with a limbo stick awaiting at the end. Doesn't matter. The morbidness of sitting in a flooded restaurant has lost its novelty, and besides, I'd really hate to be here when the next big wave hits. Breached ships can stay afloat, but everything must go perfectly to plan. It might have been sheer luck that the ship tilted the other way to tip out the water. We may not stay so lucky.

Ships are divided into watertight compartments that can be sealed off from one another. The *Titanic* was designed to stay afloat with four of its sixteen chambers filled with water; six were flooded after its steel plates were punctured, and that was enough to bring down the entire vessel in a couple of hours. The breached part of our ship must be sealed away from the rest of the ship as quickly as possible.

We form one long civilized line and spill out into the atrium, the impressive belly of the ship where a grand staircase connects two levels of shiny floors under a soaring ceiling. Mah-jongg tiles, Scrabble score sheets, glossy drink menus, and other remnants of our lives one hour earlier now litter the ground.

I walk past a man whose forehead is caked with dry blood and claim a small parcel of carpeted space between two small coffee tables that I treat like fences against my neighbors: a British couple who are doing their hardest to remain stoic and a group of six elderly American friends who are doing their best to appear cheery.

We are just a little more than half a mile from the jagged shore. It's this very proximity to the safety of land that puts us nearer to destruction and death. In 2012, the Italian cruise ship *Costa Concordia* came too close to the Isola del Giglio, off the coast of Tuscany, as Captain Francesco Schettino steered off its planned course, allegedly to impress his mistress on board. She was likely unimpressed when the eight-year-old ship tore open its hull on a shallow seabed and tipped over. For hours, passengers—the ones who didn't die, anyway—held on to railings inside the leaning tower, long after Schettino slipped into his civilian drag to escape on a lifeboat. Today, he's still serving time in prison, where, I imagine, he has significantly fewer wardrobe options.

If some passengers perished in the warm waters of the Mediterranean, what chance do we stand in this freezing storm in the North Atlantic? Photos of the half-submerged *Costa Concordia* on its side circulated the internet, and even seven years since the deadly accident, the image is clear in my head as our ship rocks side to side.

The *Viking Sky* has lowered both its anchors, neither of which is catching. Without propulsion, the ship seems to be constantly rolling the dice, banking its survival on luck. The waves are pushing us toward the shore as the terrain becomes more and more shallow.

A strange upside to being so close to land is that I have perfect Norwegian Telecom reception to replace the ship's internet, which went out with the power. To most onlookers around me, I must look like some jerk wasting what could be his last hour on earth playing Pokémon Go. I'm not.

I'm texting my family. I wish Dad good health, which is as close to I-love-you as he and I will probably ever get. Mom, on the other hand, is the rare Korean parent who'll regularly drop the L-word, either as a half-joking opening to her novella-length text messages in Korean that begin with "To my son whom I love" or simply "I love you" in English, since it can sound downright K-drama and corny in Korean. Still, I want her to hear those words in our shared language, so I try to record a voice message, except I keep screwing it up until I finally get my voice steady, as if I were recounting what I'd had for lunch. I still don't tell them that anything is amiss. As far as my parents are concerned, their son is gorging on good food and mugging for selfies with towering fjords in the distance. I don't want them to know that I'm scared.

Two years earlier (2017)

I come from effusive but private stock. We're talkers. We harp on minor annoyances and rib one another over dinner. Yet we spare the others from our deepest feelings and fears. You can say we're preserving our pride. We're also trying to protect one another.

"I have an uninvited visitor" is how Mom gave us the news of her breast cancer diagnosis in 2017. A cascade of referrals, tests, voice messages, and finally surgery followed in a matter of weeks. I canceled assignments and flew up to their Seattle suburb to become her interpreter again, as I had until I left home at eighteen. We immigrant sons grow accustomed to choosing what to translate at parent–teacher meetings; at our parents' behest, we call the insurance company and impersonate our mothers—until our voices drop, when we start impersonating our fathers. But when it came to translating Mom's oncologist appointments, I wanted to be precise and honest. I looked up words like *biopsy, lumpectomy,* and *chemotherapy* in Korean.

Mom was brassy. When her surgeon presented her with options, Mom shrugged and said, "Just cut the whole thing. It's fed three kids. It's done its job."

Her surgery was on an unusually brilliant fall day that broke a streak of Seattle's gloom. On the way to the hospital, we joked and laughed, though I can't remember about what anymore. We kept our smiles on even as the nurse's assistant wheeled her toward the operating room. Dad and I rode with her in the elevator. Only after the nurses wheeled her out and the doors began to slide shut could I let myself cry. And though I wept with relief after the surgeon came out to say all the excised lymph nodes were cancer-free, and therefore metastasis unlikely, I made sure my face was dry by the time I saw her again. I even poked fun at her when she ordered two meals—chicken teriyaki for dinner and a turkey sub to make up for the lunch she missed. That's just the way we are.

A year before I found myself aboard the drifting *Viking Sky*, in March 2018, I got to take Mom on an assignment. Or, if you want to view it more cynically, I got to use her for work. She had been talking about wanting to see New Zealand right before her cancer diagnosis, and after her surgery she took to smearing propolis—the tree sap that honeybees regurgitate to disinfect their hives—on the surgery scar. Though I was skeptical about the alleged healing powers of honey made from the nectar of New Zealand's endemic manuka plants, I thought taking Mom to the North Island's honey country would make for a good story. To do a mother-son trek on someone else's dime would make the trip all the sweeter for her, a lifelong frugalist. Mom was overjoyed. By then I thought she was back to her old self, not affected by cancer except having to take several more horse pills each day. I pitched the article to an inflight magazine and snagged us two tickets to Auckland.

We rattled down unpaved roads, visited apiaries, asked strangers to take pictures of us. We stopped for soft serves and indulged in a very generously sized panino from a roadside café that she still raves about to this day. (What is it about moms and hot sandwiches?) We made detours to places like a volcanic valley where giant leaves drooped and lichens smoldered on crusty, hot soil, and a deep-sapphire river blossomed with underwater ferns.

As all parents and children traveling together, we were bound to bicker. She fussed about the way I drove—on the other side of the road, no less—and my mood swings, which, she realized, I'd never grown out of after adolescence. I was annoyed each morning when she repacked my suitcase, dirty laundry and all, while I was in the shower. And every time she complained, which was often, I clenched my jaw until it hurt. After 500 miles of our playing Siamese twins, things came to a blow and I snapped at her for whining about the hot weather.

"Then why are you wearing black all the time?" I asked her. "And why are you always wearing heavy necklaces?"

Mom smoothed her oversize blouse and managed to smile.

"I'm trying to distract," she said. "I don't want people to notice."

She had been so brash about her surgery that I'd almost forgotten it ever happened. I thought of her—as we do of our parents—as being beyond vanity. But mastectomy isn't just about appearance. It's also about losing a part of your very being. Cancer didn't care if she wanted to forget about it and move on—it was on her mind every day. Under the black shirt and heavy necklaces I'd criticized, where her left breast used to be, there was a trench fourteen staples wide.

In that drab doctor's consultation room, she had faked being nonchalant when the surgeon asked about operation choices. It took a 7,000-mile flight and a road trip for me to understand. She had put on a brave face for her loved ones.

Now, it's my turn to do the same.

3:45 p.m.

Seventy-five knots.

Sitting in the bridge of his tugboat, Leif Arne Sørenes looks at the screen again, just to make sure he hasn't read it wrong. The wind is blowing at more than eighty-six miles per hour—well past the threshold for a hurricane. Sailing now is foolish.

Since he apprenticed on his uncle's shrimp trawler at age fifteen, Sørenes has been working at sea for more than thirty years, from the North Sea to the Gulf of Mexico to Australia's Gold Coast and back. Never has he seen this kind of weather. He's not scared of the sea; he respects it. He knows enough to sit out on a day like today. But what can you do? When the Norweigian Rescue Services requests your help, you don't say no. So Sørenes pilots the tugboat *Vivax* and his small crew into the precarious waters of Hustadvika, toward the troubled cruise ship.

At just a little over a hundred feet, the *Vivax* is less than a seventh of the length of the *Viking Sky*. But with 6,500 horsepower, the small boat is built to pull tankers and cruise ships—fitting for a scrappy boat named after the Latin word for "lively."

Vivax is not the first vessel to answer the *Viking Sky*'s call for aid, but the others—an oil tanker, a cargo ship, and a supply ship—have since given up on assisting and left. As Sørenes sees the cruise ship writhing dangerously close to shore, he has a premonition that this is about to end very badly.

Norwegian law requires local coastal pilots to go aboard cruise ships and navigate certain stretches of water, like Hustadvika. So when one of the two local pilots at the helm of the *Viking Sky* tells Sørenes "we are hanging on by a thread," he knows every second counts.

Towing a cruise ship in a storm requires a finely calibrated mix of experience and instinct. The kilometer-long steel wire has to connect just tautly enough to pull the disabled vessel but not too tight or it will snap. On a calm day, the *Vivax* could simply pick up a messenger line shot from a pneumatic line thrower on the larger ship. But for someone from the cruise ship to aim a line thrower at the small tugboat while rocking on high waves would be like hoping for a bull's eye in the dark while riding a roller coaster.

As Sørenes brings the *Vivax* alongside the *Viking Sky*, the tugboat's able seaman Bjarne Frank Nygård steps onto the deck to aim a line thrower at the cruise ship. He quickly returns, soaked. In building-height swells, being outside is suicide.

Sørenes recalls the time when he was swept overboard. He was only twenty-two, a cocksure fisherman still learning the ropes. Miraculously, the same sea that flushed him spat him right back onto the deck, slamming him against a steel beam. He spent a week in hospital, thankful that he wasn't cut in two or paralyzed for life. Then he went right back to the sea.

He's older now, more cautious. Sørenes won't let his men take chances. The crew of four hunker down inside, waiting, riding the swells.

4:10 p.m.

I know English isn't our captain's first language, but my anxiety rises when he comes back on the speaker to say, "I am *somehow* keeping the ship under control."

I'm counting on his misunderstanding the nuance of "somehow." But if he's just being his honest Nordic self, then God help us. The captain adds that a rescue is underway.

It's been almost two hours since Mayday.

The crew turn down any offer of help from some of us passengers and we stop asking. We're all liabilities, not assets. Maybe, just maybe, our overfed heft is helping; we're ballast pushing the center of gravity down. Beyond that, I don't see what we bring to the table. In fact, some of us can't wipe our own feet. I spot Ida, a housekeeper from my hallway, kneel in front of a woman whose stomach, doubled with the vest, prevents her from reaching the ground. The tiny Balinese housekeeper kneels and dries off the American's feet with a towel like Jesus in some biblical tableau.

Kurien, a waiter who's always been easy with smiles, parts the crowd like Moses, handing out cans of ginger ale.

"Don't drink too much," he jokes. "The toilets aren't flushing."

"But what's for dinner?" one of the passengers shouts back, laughing.

"It's seafood night!" the waiter quips. "Whatever you can catch."

Kurien has been the prom king equivalent of the ship, charismatic in a way that makes people believe that they've made a lifelong friend. He's not exactly a flirt, but he does have a way with his winks. Women three times his age seek him out during meal services and stop him in the hallways. Crisis or not, he can't let down his fans.

The stench of dirty dishwater fills the air. The captain announces that a tugboat has reached the ship. Moments later he returns to say the swells are making it very hard for us to connect. An hour of silence will pass before we get the same status update: One anchor. One engine. One tugboat. No dice.

Reluctantly, I call Hannes, my partner of sixteen years. It goes straight to voicemail. Should I text him? No. My hesitance isn't because I want to shield him from bad news, as I do with my parents.

Ida returns and slips a small ball of fabric to the woman whose feet she dried. As Ida walks away, the passenger tears up.

"She brought me her own stuff," she says, holding up a tiny pair of Hello Kitty ankle socks.

4:15 p.m.

As a rescue helicopter pilot, Jim H. Nielsen has two wishes when it comes to disasters: He hopes they never happen in the first place; but when one does strike, he hopes to be there to help.

Growing up on a farm in Denmark's countryside, Nielsen knew he wanted to see the world and help people. He's the big-brother type who looks after others. He joined the Royal Danish Army, then the air force, where he worked his way from air traffic control into the cockpit. Along the way he was deployed on missions in the Balkans, Iraq, and beyond. Later, he worked with the police, catching robbers and flying in antiterrorism exercises.

When he returned to civilian life, in 2007, Nielsen

took work as a helicopter pilot. Most of his flights con-
sisted of ferrying workers between Bergen and Statfjord, a vast oil field in the North Sea halfway between
Norway and Britain. Occasionally, he'd pick up a sick
crew member from an oil rig or supply ships, but those
flights seldom required him to draw on his training to
fly in even the harshest conditions.

Now, as the *Viking Sky* rocks beneath him, he posi-
tions his Sikorsky S-92 above the ship's rain-soaked
decks. The cockpit falls silent. On their one-hour
flight over from Bergen, Nielsen and his crew ban-
tered about how exciting it was to be part of a rescue mission of importance. But they hadn't realized
the scale of the mission until they arrived on scene.
Though they'd lifted one man from the deck of a supply ship in similar sea and wind conditions just the day
before, they weren't prepared for the task of moving
more than a thousand people.

Nielsen has seen ships pitch, riding waves head-on
and thumping down; he's seen them roll, swaying pre-
cariously; and he's seen them fishtail, flipping up their
rear. But he's never seen a ship do all three in a seemingly unpredictable order. One moment, the giant
cruise ship bucks like an angry horse; the next, it tips
side to side as if drunk, waves pushing and pulling its
sides. This is the stuff of sadistic Hollywood imagina-
tions, a CGI-powered scene from a disaster flick.

Most worrisome of all, the ship is wavering closer
to the shore. The dark sea breaks in white swells like a
rabid dog baring its teeth. As the water rises and falls,

reefs reveal themselves everywhere, ready to rip open the ship's halls.

Two other helicopters hover near Nielsen's. At once his cockpit fills with outside voices as the radio picks up curt, rushed sentences in Norwegian and English from every direction. The cruise ship's bridge reports trying—in vain—to secure an anchor. The Coast Guard is still trying to attach a tugboat. The helicopter pilots are trying to negotiate with the cruise crew to prepare for an evacuation.

Landing a helicopter on the ship is out of the question. Erlend Birkeland, the helicopter's rescue man, will have to attach his harness to the end of a long cable on a powerful winch, descend to the deck, strap a single passenger into a second harness, then hoist him up—while being pummeled by driving rain and gale winds. And then do that, one by one, for the rest.

In a situation like this, Nielsen thinks in steps. *Where will he position the aircraft? Where will he refuel?* But his mind can't help but wander into the murky territory where logistics overlap with ethics: What if the ship does hit one of the boulders? Would his crew immediately go to the aid of those who end up overboard, knowing that each individual rescue would take a great deal of time if Birkeland was to drop into the sea in a wet suit? Or would they continue evacuating the ship? If they knew that the ship had two hours to stay afloat, would it make sense to evacuate 120 people whose fates are uncertain, or focus on five people in the frigid sea who would perish without immediate help?

"Air traffic control to Rescue 9," a voice growls into Nielsen's headphone. "Proceed."

4:30 p.m.

The first to be airlifted off the ship are those who need medical attention. Because the elevators aren't working, the crew have to carry them in stretchers up eight flights of stairs to the helipad. Sleeves rolled up and sweat dripping off their faces, men in unbuttoned uniforms grunt in this Sisyphean parade of the infirm.

Sitting on the floor, my eyes level with theirs, I observe those who are being carried: some old, others bleeding. A woman, not old enough to collect Social Security, luxuriates on her back, grinning, and reaches out her arms to take a selfie as eight panting crew members carry her like she's a beefy Queen of Sheba. She's probably just telling her family she's okay, but I feel a surge of bile. I'm not angry just at her, but at every single one of the passengers—especially me—for being so useless.

Once the visibly weak are taken upstairs, the crew begin plucking twenty people at a time in a random order. Like a character stuck on earth in a dystopian sci-fi film, I watch them as though they were being sent to a promised land. Of course, in those Hollywood movies, the chosen ones get transported to either a high-tech idyll or an organ farm. I have no idea what awaits upstairs.

A country singer might implore me to let go and let Jesus take the wheel. If there's nothing I can do to get off the ship faster, then I might as well sit back. Anxious is a man who thinks he has a choice to make; when you realize there's not a damn thing you can do, there's peace in resignation.

Not knowing can be a pathway to happiness. As early as March 16—just days after the *Viking Sky* embarked from Bergen—meteorologists began worrying about catastrophically low pressure swirling between Iceland and Norway. The experts didn't know exactly where it would appear, but they knew this could be a nasty storm in the making. Oblivious, we dove into buffets and soaked in thermal pools. Would we have been so carefree had we known that the atmosphere was inhaling deep and waiting to exhale just in time as we crossed back over the Arctic Circle?

4:30 p.m.

Erlend Birkeland sits on the floor of Rescue 9 and swings his legs out the rear door. His orange jumpsuit shines against the anvil-colored sea below. A 195-foot rope, laden with a heavy weight, is dropping from the helicopter toward the deck of the *Viking Sky*. Ivar

Lobrot, the winch operator, double-checks the harness around Birkeland's chest one last time and gives him the okay sign. It's time to take to the sky.

As a rescue diver, Birkeland feels drawn to the ocean. But this attraction comes with awe as well, knowing firsthand what the sea can do. Part of his regular training involves throwing out a human-shaped dummy into the sea from the helicopter and rappelling down to retrieve it. More than once, he has entered the sea at an inopportune moment, the muscular waves flipping and pushing him under. He knows too well that if he's unlucky, the wire can wrap around his neck as he tumbles deeper into the water.

Hustadvika, in particular, demands respect. Birkeland has long known the area to be among the roughest parts of the Norwegian coast, with its seemingly endless rocky islets and shallow pools. He's never had to pluck anyone out of its reef-strewn waters. He hopes today won't be his first time.

Birkeland pivots 180 degrees to face the inside of the helicopter. Knees locked and stomach tightened, he begins his descent. The wind whips his face. He's been mentally preparing for this during the hour-long flight from Bergen, but he's surprised anew. It's not fear that fills his heart, but rather a heady mix of nervousness and excitement.

When Birkeland was in his twenties, he was part of a rescue team that responded when an arsonist set a ferry ablaze. During the MS *Scandinavian Star*'s overnight journey from Oslo to Frederikshavn, Denmark, a series of fires broke out and claimed the lives of 159 out of 395 passengers and ninety-seven crew. The tragedy, still an unsolved mystery without an arrest, left an indelible mark on Birkeland. He ended up pursuing a career in nursing for a time, but he felt the tug back to this dangerous profession as the years passed. At the age of forty-seven, he traded in the stable profession of hospice nurse. At the hospice, he had been helping patients die peacefully; now, he wanted to help people live.

As he drops toward the disabled cruise ship, he sees how precarious this mission is. Even though the guideline from the helicopter is secured on the deck, landing on his two feet isn't a sure bet. The winch operator and the pilot can do their best, but the sea makes the final call. The cruise ship is swaying well over a hundred feet from side to side. If it jerks away, he could lose his footing and suspend over the sea. And if the wave churns the other way, the ship—the size of a large office building—will slam into his bones. It's up to him to land unharmed—so he can help others stay alive.

In his 1912 essay "Some Reflections on the Loss of the *Titanic*," Joseph Conrad ripped into the tabloid newspapers for making a quick buck on the tragedy. "It is with a certain bitterness that one must admit to oneself that the late RMS *Titanic* had a 'good press,'" he wrote. "The white spaces and the big lettering of the headlines have an incongruously festive air to my eyes, a disagreeable effect of a feverish exploitation of a sensational God-send."

Aboard the *Viking Sky*, I can still get four bars of coverage, so I don't have to wait for tomorrow's tabloids. Anxious for information, I make the mistake of firing up Twitter. The cyber peanut gallery is in full swing with self-appointed commentators chiding the captain for sailing straight into what they're calling a bomb cyclone. On the internet, everyone gets to play armchair meteorologist. And sailor. And mechanical engineer and navigator and logistics policy wonk and maritime lawyer. In this era of "alternative facts" cooked up by a generation of Americans brought up to believe that every opinion carries equal weight, we've begun to drown in the toxic sludge of statements that begin "I just feel that . . ." Gut feelings receive airtime equal to that of basic facts—such as, say, the earth is round and a vaccine prevents polio.

Sitting on the floor, scrolling through Twitter, I see people chiming in with their half-informed beliefs about what must be happening on board—and I'm perversely comforted. This is familiar territory, and I can use any normalcy I can get. Hell, I'd give anything to go back to the boredom of just a few hours ago.

Then, my heart sinks. I see tweets of "thoughts and prayers," Americanese for resignation and inaction. That's when you know you're royally fucked.

There are commentators who seem to know far more than the passengers do. Even before the passengers suspected something was going awry, the maritime nerds were on to us. (There are apparently devotees who track satellite data and distress calls on every watery surface on earth, looking for anomalies like ours.) Their factual reports spread just as quickly as the speculation and screenshots of our mapped trajectory, all of them bouncing around the virtual echo chamber with equal weight. That's what makes the internet so frustrating in its allure: You can't tune out because there are truths among the noise.

To paraphrase one tweet in Norwegian, "Cruise #ship #VikingSky sends #MAYDAY in stormy conditions off notorious Hustadvika, western #Norway. Helicopters and ships nearby. Possible evac. of 1300 passengers." A time-stamped map shows how we were on course, running parallel to the coast, until we made a nooselike loop and took a sharp left, perpendicular to the shoreline. This must have been when we lost power and I stripped naked.

Someone on the ship has been tweeting pictures at CNN and getting ignored. But our disaster in the making is already driving the tabloids into a frenzy in the U.K., where the yellow press isn't above hacking phones, stalking just about everyone, and hunting down a princess. I wouldn't be surprised if they began dropping paparazzi from helicopters.

An aspiring travel influencer somewhere out there, seemingly wishing he were on board to cash in on the drama, is taking a different tack. He posts a tone-deaf tweet along the lines of "Visit my blog & see photos of

47

Viking Sky's sister ship, which I toured last year! #passionpassport #yolo."

Despite myself, I click and see his smiling mug plastered all over his blog as he poses in various places on a slightly older vessel of the same model. At what point will these digital whores stop? How many likes will he get for each life lost?

A friend once observed that people enjoy staking claims on even the thinnest connections to a disaster: his own claim being watching the space shuttle *Challenger* fall apart on TV with a classmate who happened to be a nephew of the teacher who was on board. We've all heard versions of such tales: A former landlord knew someone who was on the Air France Concorde that combusted into a fireball; a cousin's boyfriend's third-grade teacher was supposed to be at the World Trade Center on the morning of 9/11 but missed her train. Seeing Twitter bystanders worked up into a froth, I feel a bit smug imagining how I'll always have a story to tell strangers in a bar—if I make it out, that is.

Viking's official Twitter, meanwhile, simply pretends the growing crisis isn't happening: *Look at this picture of cute penguins! Don't they look like they're in tuxedos? Don't forget to book our Antarctica cruise where you won't need a tuxedo because our dress code is smart casual!*

On a cruise enthusiast message board, users with avatars such as BabyBoomerLass and Cruise-Gal917 are devolving into petty squabbles, dropping pedantic cruise trivia to one-up one another while simultaneously accusing the other of spreading fake news.

"I cannot imagine that they are in muster stations. They are seven decks up, I imagine," one writes. "Where are the lifeboats?" another wants to know. "I bet the engine failed because of automation," someone else chimes in. "I just feel that the captain must have been inexperienced with Nordic weather," guesses another.

I personally believe, I am convinced, I have no doubt, I can imagine, I know in my heart, I can't help but wonder that the truth must be . . .

I sigh and turn my phone off. Are twenty-first-century humans unique in our ability to equate our fantasies with facts? Have humans only recently become this stubbornly and blissfully inoculated against reality? Or is this a necessary by-product of the foolhardy imagination that created art and landed us on the moon?

Well, here is an indisputable truth: I am on a cruise ship with 1,372 other souls, and our fate is a toss-up between disaster and non-event. There's not one thing I can do other than wait and fantasize.

⁓

From a distance, the *Viking Sky* seemed like a possessed wedding cake, swinging and turning. As Erlend Birkeland dangles above the ship, he can make out

49

through the windows a jumble of furniture, broken and tossed together. As the vessel lifts and sinks thirty feet, he has to go up and down as well. It takes awhile before he lands.

Unlike the ship's messy interior, the top deck is scrubbed of any debris. The crew must have cleaned the open space to ready for evacuation. Birkeland makes his way carefully across the deck to a door and pulls it open against the gusting winds.

Inside, passengers are crammed on the stairway in a line that snakes as far down as he can see. Several are in wheelchairs. His eyes land on an elderly man with his arm cradled in a sling and his head wrapped in a blood-soaked bandage. Just how will this man get into the helicopter?

Birkeland has to start somewhere. He takes each passenger outside onto the deck, one by one. The crashing waves, ferocious winds, and helicopters above make for a deafening soundtrack. Birkeland feels the elderly skin shivering from the shock of the cold, or maybe fear or, ever more likely, both. He slips the trembling arms through the basket sling, clasps the straps, and signals at the hoist operator. The steel cable tightens, screeches, then yanks the passenger into the sky. Those too weak to stand get winched straight from their wheelchairs, unable to walk one moment, flying the next.

One by one, Birkeland sends them aloft, as his feet struggle to grip the wet deck. The ship continues its drunken dance. It's exhausting just to stay standing.

"Don't lift your arms!" Birkeland shouts at each person as he pantomimes the action, though no one can hear him. He's sent up hundreds during the course of his military service and helicopter rescue career, but those were all soldiers or oil workers: healthy young people filling out the slings with their muscled masses. If these passengers flail, they may slip through the straps and into the ocean far, far below.

Some passengers push away at the last minute, just as Birkeland is preparing the sling, scrambling back into the known dangers of the ship rather than risking the unknown in the sky. Others turn up in bathrobes, having shed their wet clothes; they soar in the Arctic air only in undergarments, their robes flapping like a superhero's cape. One couple hold on to each other until the very last minute, embracing once more as if for the last time.

The bloodied man with the injured arm stumbles out onto the deck, disoriented. Birkeland gently teases the man's arm out of the medical sling and begins buckling him up. In pain, the man squints the one eye not obscured by his bloodied bandage as Birkeland threads the man's arms through the contraption. Birkeland can't tell for sure if this man will withstand the quick but hair-raising ascent into the sky. In the back of his mind, doubt starts spreading like a drop of blood on a fresh bandage. They could save a thousand people but, he knows, if they lost just one soul, he would be haunted by that memory.

"I'm coming with you," Birkeland shouts, and clips himself alongside the man. The cable should withstand much more than the weight of both even in the gale-force wind. He pulls the frail man tight against his body, encircling his ropy arms around the passenger's torso and locking his feet behind the man's shaky legs. Their faces are close enough to feel the other's breath. Birkeland smiles, even more broadly than before, to tell the man everything will be all right. Like that, each holding on to the other in a strange embrace, the two men soar into the darkening sky.

5:13 p.m.

Even on a blue-sky day with calm seas, running a cruise involves choreography that puts any Broadway production to shame. Amid the uncertainty of possibly sinking, the ship is still a regimented troupe of several hundred who are scurrying around, tidying up and feeding us.

A pattern quickly becomes apparent. One crew member, usually North American or European, is assigned to look after a cluster of a few dozen passengers.

The concierge for my corner is Ceri, a Welshwoman who led us in the crocodile walk earlier.

"What's your job on a normal day?" I ask. I'm secretly hoping she'd ask me about my job, too, so I can tell her I'm not one of *them*, those one-percenters she's paid to babysit.

"Actually, I'm one of the two female vocalists," she says.

I mutter something about not recognizing her without makeup. I don't want her to know that I have never been to any of her nightly performances at the theater.

She doesn't seem to care. One moment, she was channeling her best Sally Bowles on stage in theatrical SparkNotes of *The Cabaret*, and the next she's directing a sea of elderlies in life vests.

Ceri would have made a great kindergarten teacher, humoring and praising us for doing the most simple tasks: "Well done, yes. One step at a time—fantastic. You're doing really, really well," she compliments a man she's propping up as he limps toward the toilet. "Oh, he's so strong, isn't he? He's the one who's holding *me* up!"

Ceri is also an interpreter. She translates our rambling, needy wishes into quick imperatives.

"You see, I think I have to let my daughter know that I'm okay," says one passenger, "but my phone doesn't seem to be working, and the screen is blank, so I just don't know . . ."

"You'd like your phone charger," Ceri says. "May I have your cabin number?"

She writes down the information and hands the

53

slip of paper to one of the speed-walkers who always boomerang back to her.

"Does anybody need medicine fetched from their cabin?" Ceri asks.

"Honey, look around," quips an older woman, sweeping her arm at the hall full of white heads. "We're *all* on medication."

The ship, too, is sick. It moans as the sea slaps and twists it from all directions. The elevator shafts, once noiseless, howl in a haunting tone I'm certain will return in my dreams. Distracted by the constant chamber music and smooth jazz, we forget that a ship is like a living being, gassy, noisy, and sometimes incontinent. Now, with nothing masking the sounds, I hear the ship losing decorum and control. I feel it deteriorating.

We don't hush one another or stop mid-sentence anymore when the PA system turns on. The captain tells us the propulsion system is functioning, and one of the two anchors has finally caught. But if that were meant to cheer us up, it doesn't. At least he omitted that we'd come close to capsizing. Months later, in an interview with Norway's most widely read daily newspaper, a professor of marine engineering will estimate that the ship's keel could have been as close as sixteen inches from meeting the underwater rocks at one point. NRK, the national broadcaster of Norway, estimates that we came about 100 yards away from grinding against the ten-foot-shallow seabed.

"Again, we are somehow keeping the ship under control," the captain says.

Under her breath, the English passenger next to me mutters "Shit"—the first word I've heard her speak. Her husband turns to her, horrified. They quickly return to looking emotionless.

6:12 p.m.

"Why did the engines fail?" Hannes barks into the phone in his native German, his voice groggy from sleep. "Why aren't you on a lifeboat?"

Whereas I often respond to challenges with sadness ("Ach, you and your depression!" Hannes would say), my partner of sixteen years wields anger like a weapon whenever confronted with something that displeases him.

Because he's so addicted to CNN, I figured he would be well up to speed by now. But it's a little past nine o'clock on Saturday back home in San Francisco, which means he's in bed if he's home in our apartment. He might be irritable because I've woken him up. I shouldn't have called.

Hannes was twenty-two when met, a lovable curmudgeon with a tender inner life I felt privileged to see. He was still grieving his mother, who'd passed away from breast cancer a couple of years before; he avoided his sadness then by pouring himself into his biochemistry studies. I was fresh out of college on a professional exchange program in Germany, where I ended up picking up most of the language from him.

"It's fine. Nobody's seriously hurt," I say, in German. "There are helicopters evacuating passengers, and they're even feeding us."

He curses at the incompetence of everyone, working himself up into his own cycle of rage. I know it's not directed at me—it may even be that he's scared—but I still flinch at each outburst.

In the past seven years, since we moved from Berlin to San Francisco, Hannes has become an unceasingly angry man. In the soap opera version of our relationship, my character would cock his chin and lob a cliché: "I don't even know who you are anymore." But life's no TV show. Standing so close, I've lost perspective. Just as we can't see in the morning mirror how we gradually wrinkle or grow lumpy, I don't realize how different we've become except when I look back at our years in Germany and remember we used to be happy.

That's how life works, isn't it? Before a storm rises, air pressure drops without our bodies sensing change. A furious earthquake may be the symptom that flattens cities, but it's the unnoticeable crawl of tectonic plates that causes the earth to snap and rupture. The mightiest of changes are taking place when we barely register them.

I really dodged a bullet by not bringing him on this trip, as I have on a handful of assignments. He's a great travel-mate when things go well; when he's unwell, he makes sure that those around him are, too.

He gets more worked up on the phone when I can't answer his rapid-fire questions about the ship's shortcomings or the order of evacuation. All I can do is assure him everything's just fine. Why is it that those in the midst of a crisis must often take on the extra burden of soothing others? Hannes exhausts me.

"I have to go," I lie. "My phone's running out of battery."

6:34 p.m.

When the sea swells with rage, docked cargo ships and reinforced piers become hazards to one another; some ports even force the bulky vessels to leave when a hurricane approaches. Made for the sea, container ships cut through the waves farther into the ocean in bad weather, rather than duck away toward land. The open water may be the safest place for a large ship during a storm.

The freighter *Hagland Captain*, loaded with heavy timber, was sailing north in the opposite direction when the MV *Viking Sky* issued the distress call. As rain and sea mist clouded visibility, the 100-yard-long cargo ship changed course and motored toward the coast in hopes of helping the cruise ship.

The International Maritime Organization, a United Nations agency working with the shipping industry, requires mariners to aid one another: "A master of a ship at sea, which is in a position to be able to provide assistance on receiving a signal from any source that persons are in distress at sea, is bound to proceed with all speed to their assistance."

But the moral code that guides mariners certainly goes back further than the United Nations and, perhaps, any written charters or signed treaties. Fishermen and sailors have gone out of their way to save one another for as long as humans have taken to bodies of water. Maybe that makes the sea the most human environment after all: it distinguishes a person from an animal, for what is more human than to reach out, even risking one's own survival, on behalf of another? That we can lend a hand in a time like this might just prove humanity exists; It may prove that we're not on this planet merely to propagate.

As the *Hagland Captain* speeds toward us—"speed" being a relative term here, of course—the ocean's pent-up rage erupts in waves as tall as hills that collapse as quickly as they form, as if vacuumed up, only to rise again with more ferocity. If land is a slow and steady giant moving at a glacial pace, water is a hot-tempered monster, creating and erasing topography in a matter of seconds: What is a mesa turns into a valley that sends us tumbling down its steep sides.

Water can turn into quicksand, too.

The same sea that has trapped the *Viking Sky*

grips the *Hagland Captain* in a tightening vise. As the freighter plunges and tries to fight the maelstrom, its engines stall. At 4,599 tons of deadweight (or the total carrying capacity), the *Hagland Captain* can weigh more than ten Boeing 747s. Without propulsion, however, it's spun and tossed like a balsa-wood plane in a tornado.

Minutes after seven o'clock, the *Hagland Captain* suffers the same fate as the *Viking Sky*. All is dark. Its engines are dead. The ship lists helplessly, unleashing a torrent of timber from the deck into the sea like a burst bag of toothpicks.

The cargo ship's captain, Nils Kristiansen, takes to the radio.

"Mayday-mayday-mayday, this is *Hagland Captain*," he shouts. "We are capsizing."

Inside the cockpit of Rescue 9, Jim H. Nielsen usually speaks a mix of his native Danish and his colleagues' Norwegian. But when he hears the *Hagland Captain*'s Mayday, he blurts out the only thing he can think to say, in English.

"Really?"

His copilot, Stian Nagelsen, nods in confirmation. It *is* happening. When the helicopter reaches the *Hagland Captain*, the freighter is listing at forty-five degrees while Hustadvika's waves lick one side of the deck as if hungry. The lead-colored sea swallows the cargo of logs, then spits them out against the freighter.

Rescue man Birkeland squeezes into a wet suit.

Only moments ago, Nielsen felt at least a modicum of control. The helicopter had just dropped off its first twenty passengers at a community gym–turned–makeshift Red Cross center, refueled, and lifted off to return to the *Viking Sky*. Nielsen felt the calming tunnel vision he gets during an evacuation: one thing at a time, each done with precision.

Now, the freighter has thrown everyone for a loop. There are only nine men aboard the *Hagland Captain*, but the situation is much deadlier. The ship is not only violently moving and quickly capsizing, but also being battered by the loose logs that ram its hull like spears launched from a torpedo tube.

The sky turns dusky. Nielsen beams his searchlight onto the ship. From above, the crew of nine look like ants being pelted by a garden hose, scrambling around the red deck. An anchor is dropped in vain. The ship keeps drifting toward the minefield of reefs.

Nielsen stays above the *Hagland Captain* for forty minutes before another helicopter comes to relieve him so he can head back to the *Viking Sky*.

Later, Nielsen hears the captain of another helicopter radio the crew of the *Hagland Captain*: "To the bow! Go to the front of the ship and jump!"

Imagine having to choose between staying on a capsizing ship and jumping into the ocean—between risking it all and risking it all.

The crew members of the *Hagland Captain* follow Captain Nils Kristiansen's order to abandon ship. The only way out is through the water that surrounds them.

They tie one end of a long rope to a cleat, just as they've done hundreds of times. But today, they're not securing the ship onto a dock. They're securing their lives.

The nine crew members gather forward. Except for the Norwegian captain, they are all a long way from home: Ukraine, Estonia, the Philippines. Having signed up for a life at sea, perhaps they've already made peace with the possibility of dying far from their loved ones.

One by one they launch, holding on to the rope, holding on to the hope that they'll keep their heads above water long enough for a rescuer to fish them out.

8:37 p.m.

"One of the rescue helicopters had to be rerouted to help another vessel" is the *Viking*

Sky captain's vague update. "Currently we have two helicopters assisting us." In our bubble, we are spared the stink of guilt—this is not a group ready to process knowing that saving our lives might be costing others'.

I lose track of time in the bright atrium. I'd believe it if someone told me it was three o'clock or ten, morning or evening. The captain updates us again: Two helicopters. One willing but unable tugboat. One anchor. Wait, didn't we already hear this?

Adrenaline gives way to boredom. The new normal becomes déja vu: Ceri takes down orders like an old-school apothecary; her Filipino and Indonesian helpers return with pouches; somewhere, a passenger complains of wet feet. In our uneasy confinement, time is a Mobius strip, never ending and always repeating.

I look around for a traveler named Mary.

Mary is a roadrunner of a human, long-necked and twitchy, willing to run you over if you don't get out of the way. We met on the first day while waiting in line to check in and have run into one another several times since. At each encounter, she talked a mile a minute while pointing out, again and again, that this was her first cruise.

"I mean, I thought it would be a convenient way to see the northern lights, but I just never travel in packs like this," she said, cocking her head at the crowd all slightly older than she was. "I'm definitely not going on any of the group excursions. I booked a private trip with a local guide at each port."

Deep down, I think, she's insecure about inching

closer to 60 and becoming one of *those* people, folks who appreciate the comfort and safety of this sailing. I wince a bit as I see in Mary my own conflicted unease meets hypocrisy. While Mary and I balk at the idea of telling our friends—without irony or an air of superiority—that we willingly came on this cruise, haven't we actually enjoyed the climate-controlled environment where all we need to do is chew? Aren't we relieved, after a day of dropping in on the local scenery for a few hours, when we return to the same bed each night without having to lift our bags once, all our stuff neatly sorted in drawers?

I'll admit—and I'll throw Mary under the boat here, too, I guess—that by being here, we're cruise people.

Why must I always stand a bit outside the dotted line, always looking, pulled by my curiosity but never willing to let go and jump in?

Until a couple of days ago, we sailed calm seas through intricate channels paneled by snow-blanketed mountains so white they glowed cool blue long after sunset. Sometimes we floated toward impressive landmasses with chiseled peaks; other times we were suddenly out in the open sea, bobbing at the uncertainty of a blank horizon.

Why on earth did humans continue moving north, past the Arctic Circle? And more important, why did they ever stop to settle there? As we navigated past snow-sprinkled islets and moss-covered rocks, I would sometimes spot a red farmhouse, planted alone on an outcrop in the middle of nowhere. I couldn't fathom what it would feel like to exist just a couple of feet above the ocean, surrounded by fickle winds and rough waves. In the months when the sun refuses to come out, do the inhabitants delight in this quiet?

Looking out at the silent landscape from the deck of our slowly passing cruise ship yesterday, I wondered how someone accustomed to that kind of raw aloneness would fare on a crowded cruise ship like this.

And how long would these gregarious cruisers, who crave and thrive in the company of strangers, endure in a remote place like that?

I couldn't imagine lasting very long at either of these extremes. My whole life has been a push-pull between the polar needs for aloneness and for companionship. Being in this ship's atrium with hundreds of people now makes me feel lonelier than I have felt all week. But I'm not sure if I'd feel better being out in a remote farmhouse, all by myself.

Maybe Mary and I are already in the only place we know how to inhabit: among others, but never quite belonging.

9:33 p.m.

My legs are putty after hours of contorting my body into a tiny nook between two coffee tables. Bones and joints click like a computer keyboard when I get up. The sea continues to batter us at random intervals and my bladder's begun to feel like a sloshing sea inside of me. Just standing in place feels like balancing a tray of raw eggs with an inflatable bouncy castle. But I can't hold it any longer. I've got to go.

The state of the men's room shocks me. Everything is gleaming under the bright light, and there's a hint of citrus in the air. The door clicks behind me, and the busy chatter and the howling of elevator shafts stop in an instant, as if all unapproved sounds are sucked out. Instead, birdsong spills out of invisible speakers.

Did I just walk through a portal to a different world, one far from this busted ship?

Peeing while wearing a bulky flotation device poses a new challenge in coordination. I fumble with my pants and pull out my passport from the underwear. I can't see below my upper chest. Though I'm pretty confident with my aim, the prospect of missing the urinal makes me sweat a little. I don't want to soil this immaculate room, wiped down to factory condition. As I back away from the urinal, I half expect a cleaner on duty to drop from the ceiling, wielding sanitizing spray.

But there's no ninja housekeeper. Just invisible birds chirping without a pause.

I wave my hand under the faucet to see if the sensor works. Brown water gushes out, and the sight of it reminds me that I'm not crazy: What you see isn't always the truth. The staff can keep buffing the surface, but everything is breaking down beyond the skin of this capsule.

Outside, I walk through a cloud of strangers' conversations, which hang in the air like a respiratory virus I have to inhale.

". . . I caught my then-husband cheating, so what could I . . ."

". . . we produce contemporary Christian pop music festivals around . . ."

". . . because it's such a good time to refinance, we thought . . ."

Anniversary. Friends' reunion. Retirement. Annual holiday. Mom-and-daughter bonding. There are many reasons why people came on this cruise. Stories, as they do, take erratic turns and lead to other unexpected tales. How random is it that these divergent paths of our lives should converge at all? I'm learning intimate stories about people whose names I may never know.

"Hey, man, how've you been?"

It's Peter Bohler, the travel photographer whom I met just a few days ago; he's one of the few non-staffers on the ship who's my age. I'm so overjoyed to see a familiar face that I almost hurl my body into his for a bear hug. No, better not. With our boxy vests, we'll knock each other out like sumo wrestlers.

Like me, Peter is here on assignment, for a different magazine from the one I'm currently supposed to be writing for. It's actually the very same magazine that just sent me on the earlier cruise from Bali.

Freelancing requires professional promiscuity, and I feel a little dishonest, betrayed, and jealous all at once in a situation like this, as if I were in an open relationship and just ran into my boyfriend's date, who's more successful than I am.

No matter. Peter and I share the affinity of being creative mercenaries. While disembarking at a port a few days ago, we spotted each other easily, recognizing the here-for-business stares and notepad-in-the-pocket gait of freelancers. Since then, we've shared a few meals and exchanged text messages. We're bonded in our strange status as imposter passengers, caught somewhere between the upstairs and the downstairs of this hierarchical world: Yes, we know we don't belong, but we're still coddled like any other passenger, waiting to be airlifted.

"What a day," Peter says.

"Tell me about it," I say.

"Do you think our assignments will get killed?" he asks, looking bummed.

"If we don't get killed first," I say.

We laugh because that's the only thing left to do.

In some ways, we're two dinosaurs trying to evolve into birds. As the print media entered the current ice age, we've watched the craft we've worked years to hone—respect for our subjects, thoughtful composition, careful editing—become almost worthless in favor of the lightning speed of social media. Sure, we've adapted as well as we could, but reluctantly. So instead of snapping away quick shots and selling them right now to the highest bidders online, Peter keeps his camera in the case.

Before the ship's alarm had sent the day into chaos, Peter and I had met up in the Explorers Lounge. After the trivia quiz, as the storm doubled down, we stepped out onto the deck, not knowing how foolhardy we were being. Gusts slapped us so hard they nearly stripped our glasses from our faces. He asked me to grab him by his jacket as he leaned into the storm, ski jumper–style, to take pictures of the sea. Stumbling inside, we had to join forces to pull the door shut. As we stood just inside the closed door, a crew member came running and posted a sign forbidding passengers to go outside.

It all seemed like an adventure back then; what a difference half a day makes.

"Have you backed up all your stuff?" I ask.

Peter pats his pants, nervously.

"I have some of my memory cards," he says. "But my hard drive is in my cabin."

Photographers guard their raw files like their own life. My notebooks may get swept away, combust into flame, or shred to pieces, but I could still wring scenes from my memory, redo interviews on the phone, and file a serviceable article. But photographers don't have the same luxury. When it comes to work, their memory cards count more than their true memory.

I think about my clunky laptop, still in my cabin. And my only backup drive? Right next to it. It was a genius move to bring both on the same trip. That means all my writing, more than just the source of my income, is on this ship. Aside from the freelance stuff—article ideas, drafts, clips, and invoices—I have everything else I've been trying to write. I have confided in my closest friends—but even then, only in passing and with vague references—that I want to write books. After more than a decade of doing this, I have very little to show for myself: a handful of short stories in literary magazines and countless abandoned projects.

Yet my heart beats a little faster as I think about losing it all. What would life be without my computer and backup drive? Freed from the unrevised short stories, ditched novels, and half-baked plots, I won't have a choice but to start anew. Will I shrug it off as Elizabeth Bishop pretends to in her poem "One Art"—*their loss is no disaster*—and move on? Will I go, say, work for Twitter?

The sea begins slapping the ship on the side, then shakes us violently. Peter and I lurch, gripping the banister until the floor stops tilting.

"My girlfriend told me on the phone," he says, quietly, "that she's pregnant. I haven't told anyone."

I can't think of how to respond.

"I guess I wanted to say it aloud," he says. "You know, just in case."

I nod and try to return his smile. He seems unburdened, lighter. I have to look away or I'll cry. Of all the 7.5 billion people in this world, I happen to be the one bearing witness to this man's announcement.

The corridors that encircle the atrium are packed. Every one of us, every single one of the hundreds of souls here, has left behind spaces big and small in the lives of others around the world, like reliefs that make up a frieze. We are someone's uncles and aunts and friends and lovers and mothers and fathers. And an about-to-be father.

There's a human being on their way to this world and their entire life trajectory is already at a crossroads: they may have a dad who regales them with stories from his assignments around the globe; or they may be left with nothing but photographs to know him by.

I've been so wrapped up in what *I* could lose that I have neglected to consider my nieces and nephew, my parents, my sisters, my friends. What do they stand to lose?

No, I'm not about to fall into an *It's a Wonderful Life* reverie, but I'm not going to lie, either: I tear up.

"We'll be okay," Peter says.

"Yeah, we're going to be fine," I say, just as unconvinced.

10:10 p.m.

What does Hannes stand to lose?

We have spent most of our twenties and thirties together. We've become messy vines that entangled as they scaled a wall. Separating us would mean altering the very organisms of us—if it's possible at all.

We back up each other's memories; we've seen each other grow up. He'd lose that. He'd also lose a respectable partner—*A travel writer? How exotic!*—who cracks up his colleagues with self-deprecating stories at dinner parties prepared pretentiously with ingredients from faraway trips. He'd also lose the comfort of knowing there's one person who's always had his back. Hannes would lose his biggest believer.

What does he stand to gain if I don't make it out of here?

He won't have someone nagging at him for putting off chores. He'd never have to clean up after me again, picking up half-full mugs, piles of clementine peels, bushels of black hair, and books opened to random pages that I get mad at him for closing. Most of all, he'd gain the freedom he craves. As difficult as a separation would be, I understand his craving. I always bring my backup drive on trips because part of me hopes I'll disappear.

I settle back in the nook between the stoic Brits and the cheerful American retirees and dial Hannes. He picks up, then switches on the video. The connection is slow. He fills my screen, fuzzy and discolored. I can make out his wraparound sunglasses hiding his eyes; I can see the car seat belt across this chest. Then, for a few seconds, everything comes into sharp focus. Next to his face, through the driver's-seat window, the brilliant California sun illuminates a cluster of restaurant signs in Chinese. Above his stubble, his mouth looks . . . lined in black.

"What the fuck?" I blurt out in English, startling my neighbors, before switching to our usual German. "Did you just eat Dan Dan noodles? Did you *really* go to the Szechuan place on Irving?"

"I was hungry!" he says. "How did you know?"

Fine, I didn't expect him to sit at home and light up votives while praying to gods he doesn't believe in. And I didn't want him glued to CNN, biting his fingernails bloody. Still, it smarts to see him carry on as though it's a regular lazy Saturday and nothing's amiss. I wanted him to at least lose his appetite out of worry for my life.

"Check your mirror," I say. "You're *dégueulasse*."

Early on in our relationship, we decided to use French—the language he and I both took in school—for uncomfortable words. Everything in French sounded fancy, we agreed, and therefore more suitable for unpleasantries and vulgarities. So instead of speculating that a friend needed to stop being a moody tight-ass by getting laid, we'd call him *mal-baisé*. Instead of calling each other *widerlich*, or disgusting, we took to saying *dégueulasse*, jokingly. We speak a private Esperanto, made by and for only us.

Hannes checks the mirror, wipes his mouth, and starts laughing. "Leave me alone!"

I chuckle, too. My heart's breaking.

Across the aisle, a silver-haired couple lean against

each other, swaying as if at a reunion dance. The woman, who's shorter, rests her arms and forehead on the ledge of the man's life jacket.

This. This is what Hannes and I stand to lose. A chance to lean on each other in a crisis. A future in which we'll continue comforting each other in a language of our making.

The time has come for one particular couple to be winched up into the helicopter. They've spent the last four hours standing in the windowless staircase, waiting. Finally, they are at the front of the line.

The man looks bewildered. Several times he's tried to wander off but his wife has herded him back to the line, whispering into his ear things nobody else can hear.

The door opens, shocking them with the cold. A uniformed crew member takes the man's arm and his wife clutches the other arm. The crew has to hold her back. There's no time to waste.

She follows them outside and shouts. She tries to tell them that she must go with him, that he's scared, that he doesn't understand. That he has Alzheimer's.

Nobody can hear her. The rescuer puts her husband, who's babbling and gesturing wildly, into the sling. The last strap snaps shut. The cable tightens. Into the opaque sky he disappears.

Sometime in the night

"So, did you enjoy the helicopter ride?" asks Dad on the phone. "Are you settled in your hotel room?"

"What?"

"Viking called," says Dad. "They said you were evacuated. You're at the Hotel—hang on, I wrote it down."

Dad speaks the combative southeastern dialect of Korean that makes his sentences rise and fall like an angry sea. Tonight, he sounds worried—even soft.

"*Guenchana*?" Mom cuts in. "Are you okay?"

"I'm fine," I say.

"What an ordeal!" she says. "Were you scared? It's in the news. They say a lot of passengers are still on the ship."

"Um . . . I'm one of them."

She takes a sharp breath. "What? They said they rescued you."

Someone, maybe a Red Cross volunteer, must have accidentally crossed my name off the ship's manifest.

"Don't worry," I tell Mom sheepishly, knowing exactly what she's about to ask. "There's plenty to eat."

"I don't understand," she says. "Why haven't they taken you?"

"It's random," I say.

"Those geriatrics have already lived their best lives!" she says. "They should be airlifting the young ones!"

"I don't think that's how it works," I say. "If anything, I think the oldest passengers get taken off first."

74

"I should have come with you," she says.

My chest tightens at the thought of my seventy-four-year-old diabetic, cancer-surviving mother with weak knees believing she could save me.

"Ha! As if you could help," I tease her, because that's the way we know to keep our voices steady, she and I.

"If they're going by age, I'd go up to them and demand a seat in the helicopter," she says. "So I can give it to you."

I'm 6'3", thirty-nine years old, and still her baby.

"Don't worry," I say, extra cheerful. "They're about to serve dinner. I'll text you."

Ceri comes around with cookies and apples. She's reprising her role as our kindergarten teacher. *Well done! Look at this! Oh, that's just wonderful,* she coos in a lilting accent.

In between the acts, her face darkens, like the rest of us. Because most announcements fall into the category of "We are *somehow* okay" or "No news is good news," the crew are turning to their telephones for updates.

Ceri's brother and her fiancé have been texting her every few minutes; that's when she breaks character and sighs quietly. There's more news from her loved ones than she lets on.

In an alternate timeline, in which the engines didn't inexplicably shut down, we would be riding these high waves forward. Ceri would be backstage warming up her voice for tonight's performance—*The Greatest Hits of ABBA*, was it?—rehearsing her pivots and turns and shimmies. The passengers would be finishing poached salmon and *poulet de Bresse*, their most pressing dilemma being: crème brûlée or Success Cake? We'd file into the Star Theater, where the chairs form a half-moon facing the stage, and sip our gin and tonics as Ceri and three other performers burst into the spotlight: *Mamma Mia!*

Instead, the Star Theater, being one of the two muster stations, is packed with half of the ship's passengers, not a single catchy Euro pop tune to be heard. And the other half of us are littered here across the atrium like discarded menus that the vigilant crew's forgotten to clean up sometime in the night.

"Well, my agent booked me," Ceri says when one of her charges asks how she came to be a cruise entertainer. I want to blurt out, *Do you hate him?*

The way life works, I think, is a series of coin tosses and dice throws that lead us down one path out of an infinite number of possibilities. What if Ceri had said no to her agent on that balmy spring day? (I don't know why—I picture her in a summer dress and denim jacket outside a used bookstore on some cobblestone street, excited to see her agent's name flash across her phone screen.) If she had only tapped "decline" on that call, maybe today she'd be on stage playing Cosette in the never-ending West End production of *Les Misérables*; or pulling espresso shots for thankless bankers in the lobby of a Cardiff skyscraper; or touring Europe, performing avant-garde theater pieces that involve an inordinate amount of screaming.

What if she had thrown in the towel and gone back to school for medicine? Maybe she'd be in an NIH clinic somewhere dreary, wishing she were on a cruise.

And me? What if Ron, the mercurial editor of the travel magazine that sent me here, had never called?

Ron is notorious among freelance writers for his mood swings: one day as cloying as a Southern lady sipping sweet tea, then barking self-esteem-destroying dismissives the next. I've known more than one writer he's brought to tears, and I was on the receiving end of his verbal face slaps when I deigned to pitch him a story that he deemed to be so egregiously beneath his publication that he felt compelled to call and yell at me.

Ron emailed me six months ago while I was on assignment in Fiji. Without elaborating, he wrote that he urgently needed to speak with me. As in all abusive relationships, I wasn't sure if I was about to get a browbeating or a "Baby, I love you!" I dropped everything to hike to a resort bar with reliable Wi-Fi—and was relieved to find him more Jekyll than Hyde when I answered the Skype call. And when he asked "How would you like to go on a northern lights cruise?" I didn't hesitate for a second and thanked him profusely.

Now—sharing this eye-blinding atrium with a man who's going to be a father, a housekeeper who gave away her last Hello Kitty socks, a classically trained cellist directing foot traffic, a Welsh actress playing au pair—I'm thinking *What if*? What if I'd said no? What if Don had called that day to yell at me rather than assign me a story about the northern lights? What if the Wi-Fi had failed that day in Fiji so he'd been forced to give the story to some other sucker who would be on this ship in my place?

Two days before the storm

A more superstitious man might wonder if we jinxed ourselves into a deadly situation by crossing off an item that's on most travelers' bucket list. A few nights ago—though it feels like another lifetime now—I saw the northern lights for the very first time. They were more beautiful than I'd hoped, yet more fleeting than I'd imagined. The green boomerang moved up and down the sky—not exactly a dance but more like an outdated Shinjuku neon light, flickering in five different spots as if programmed before extinguishing itself. It couldn't have lasted more than a few seconds.

To see the lights, I'd joined a caravan of behemoth tour buses that awaited at the port of Tromsø, a university town above the Arctic Circle once lauded as the "Paris of the North." From this hillside city of clapboard-sided homes and snow-covered streets, the buses took hundreds of tourists into the dark folds of the surrounding mountains.

The forecast wasn't great: Clouds were closing in, and the solar activities that cause the northern lights appeared unpromising. The night air turned my face into a block of ice that cracked a little with each exhalation and refroze with every intake of painful breath. I was among busloads of gawkers in the middle of a valley—a popular cross-country-skiing site during the day, I was told—turning in sync each time someone shouted *Look over there!*

A cruise is perfect preparation for viewing the northern lights because they both require interminable waiting. Turn up for the daily excursions, then wait in a lightless theater replaying TED Talks. When the guide funnels you to the hallway, exit and wait. Get corralled down a gangway and move so gingerly that you might as well be standing still. Bottleneck through a gate. Stand around some more to get on the bus. Nod while learning all about your neighbor's very accomplished grandkids. Drive for ten minutes or an hour. Then wait some more to get off the bus.

Waiting becomes more than second nature; it becomes the very core of your being. And patience is a necessary virtue if you want to catch the northern lights.

Auroras are like paint flecks, the result of the sun spitting electrons and protons. Together they stream toward the earth through the vacuum of space for three days before they strike our atmosphere. The sun's charged spittle combusts with the earth's gaseous atmosphere in bright spectacles near the magnetic poles. As I saw those green shimmers, rippling sixty miles above my head, they seemed at once distant and so close: an optical illusion of the grandest scale.

Before Photoshopped photos and CGI movies left us jaded, humans tried to explain these surreal phenomena as red fox, dragons, whale's plumes, the coming of the French Revolution, and spirits fighting while being egged on by humans. Among these stories, I like the local lore from the Sámi, the nomadic residents of the Arctic Circle, the most: The crackling sound, which you hear when the light show is especially strong, is said to be the dead trying to speak to you.

"Whether that's true or not, who knows?" said Karen, a Sámi woman I'd met earlier that day. "It's certainly a nice thought when you're alone in the mountains."

Before seeing the northern lights, I went on an excursion called *The* Sámi Experience, whose essentialist title made me uneasy. It turned out to be one of the cruise's highlights. Sure, it was well-oiled tourist machinery that put visitors through the rehearsed sequence of an open fire, a short talk on the Sámi culture, then a ride by a single poor reindeer pulling a chain of sleighs carrying tourists. But Karen made a charming host, together with her husband, Roar. They entertained us in their outpost of cabins and a hotel made of blocks of ice far out in Tamok Valley, a vast area with fewer than eighty year-round inhabitants. The white peaks of the Lyngen Alps were obscured by clouds closing in on us, bringing more March snow.

In a colorfully knitted shawl and furry boots,

rosy-cheeked Karen was the picture of the Arctic life we see in magazines. But she's hardly a Luddite—when I wandered off from the group, she ended up fetching me on her snowmobile.

A reindeer needs six years of training before it acquiesces to human commands, and then puts in ten years of hard work before it's slaughtered for meat. Sámi herders remain seminomadic in this era of smartphones and air travel, moving the beasts hundreds of miles north to the winter camp, where, counterintuitively, colder weather means better foraging for the animals, thanks to the edible greens hiding under the more abundant and fluffier snow.

When he's not helping his wife entertain tourists, Roar travels for months at a time, protecting the herd from eagles, lynx, and wolverines. Natural predators aside, climate change has created new hazards for Sámi herders. Last fall, the snow did not arrive on time, which meant the herders had to wade across rivers with the animals, rather than gliding over frozen ice as they have through history.

When *The* Sámi Experience ended and our tour bus pulled away, I waved back at Karen and Roar, imagining them jonesing to get higher up in the mountains, away from us needy tourists and into that utter aloneness surrounded by nothing but snow, reindeer, and the northern lights.

Now, sitting in this ship's messy atrium, I think of them. I imagine them stoking an open fire to boil tea and cranking up a transistor radio. Wait. Who am I kidding? They're probably scrolling through Facebook on their smartphones. When Karen and Roar happen on the news item about the adrift cruise ship, will they know that they met some of the passengers a few days ago? Will they speak back to the northern lights and ask the ghosts to watch over us?

10:23 p.m.

By now, journalists are circling around the handful of Twitter users on the ship for exclusive scoops: "Follow me so I can DM you!" "Email me at . . ." "What's a good number 4 U"

A more entrepreneurial freelancer would be making videos and looking for the highest bidder. He'd take pictures of broken glass glittering on soggy carpet, collect sound bites from distraught grannies, and tweet out minute-by-minute updates. Maybe I can whip up a Buzzfeed shitpost real quick: *Seven Times When I Thought I Was Dead Aboard a Luxury Cruise and Wasn't Even Mad About It: Sponsored Content in Partnership with Expedia.*

If I felt like an entitled bro, I might swagger into the staff-only area of the ship with a camera and go all *Vice* on them: *We go undercover into the bowels of a luxury cruise ship carrying thousands to their watery graves!*

How about some puns for a *New York Post* headline? *A Salt Weapon: Buoy, Are They in Trouble!*

I *am* taking pages and pages of notes, even though I have no endgame in mind. I don't want to hawk these tidbits to the tabloids; I've spent too many years peddling words like goods. I begin to feel that what I'm witnessing tonight might lead to a story worth telling with more care. And a story, ripened under the dirt of the consciousness, can ferment into something delicious or even medicinal. Maybe this story could heal me someday.

The cheery staff bounce on the balls of their feet, carrying platters of fruit, cheese, and even maki sushi bursting at their sides. We're lost at sea, but the kitchen is still sending out overstuffed crab rolls. I want to curl up into the fetal position from the fatigue but force myself to swallow a piece of avocado roll, the luke-warm mayo coating my mouth. The food makes me thirstier; I've sweated through all the layers I piled on more than eight hours ago. But then I'd have to drink, which would mean going back to the bathroom, and the whole cycle repeats.

Bodily functions are so inconvenient in times of crisis, or, for someone like my grandmother, when traveling in general. When my family speak of my father's mother, we shake our heads and smile about how she refused to drink a drop of water all day when-ever she traveled; she would even avoid soup for days beforehand. My grandmother's aversion to public toi-lets—a random legacy that skipped a generation to me—was as great as her fear of getting on the wrong bus at the rest stop.

I'm trapped on a cruise ship in Norway, yet thinking of someone who passed away twenty-some years ago in Korea. Why do we hold on to such odd trivia about loved ones long gone? Is it some warped form of love to fondly recall someone's eccentricities? What strange, slightly embarrassing bits will I be remembered for?

We have entered the ninth hour since the power blinkered out. The moaning of metal has become our constant soundtrack. Against that low, dull sound I can hear the unnerving clanging of an errant champagne bucket rolling around the marble floor of the level just below us. When I refresh my web browser, the Norwegian state broadcaster reports that 130 passengers have been safely helicoptered to land. I do some quick math. At this rate, it will take sixty hours to get all of us out of here. Sixty. Hours. Two and a half days.

"We have a lot of sea, as you can see," says the captain. "For now, we do have control over the ship."

I appreciate a dry sense of humor as much as the next guy, but the good captain really needs to stop saying things like "for now" and "somehow."

Three of the four engines are back up and running. Yet they're not enough to help us outrun the gales, now almost halved to forty knots but still considered gale force enough to veer a car on the road. Just when I think we'll be all right, the ship plunges and rolls. The captain tells us that a couple of tugboats are still trying—and failing—to connect as we struggle to stay away from land.

Darkness has long filled the portholes. The chandelier in the atrium feels brighter, harsher. Kurien, the jokester waiter, comes by with a red biohazard bag to collect trash. "Ho, ho, ho, Santa's here," he shouts. "But you've all been bad so he's taking away your soda cans."

From down below, a crystal-clear voice rings out, first quietly, then gaining strength. I learn from the other passengers that this is the female vocalist who shares the stage with Ceri each night. A trim, dark-haired woman stands in one corner of the atrium, facing the audience of hundreds and belting out Leonard Cohen's "Hallelujah." Everyone's so polite, but I want to scream: *Too soon, girl, we're not dead yet!*

It's way premature for a postmortem. Stop singing that funeral song. Stop.

Oh, fine, "Hallelujah" does get to me, damn it. But I'm not imagining my own memorial service. Instead, my head is filled with pictures of me and Hannes together.

We used to be so disgustingly in love that we might have even described ourselves as *dégueulasse* once or twice. In the memorial slide show in my mind, I see a snapshot of us taken at Legoland and developed at the local drugstore. We're two gangly twenty-two-year-olds grinning in front of a country western–themed saloon built out of Lego blocks. Look at us when he started graduate school—pimples still covered my forehead and Hannes still had hair. Remember Sardinia, and how we scored nineteen-euro tickets from Berlin, then drove around the whole island in a dented car from a dubious rental place and almost got stuck in a freak snowstorm. Think—fondly—of that screaming match we had in front of a rusty roller coaster in Yangon, when he was too concerned for my safety to let me go: Even though I love going on rides alone and he hates roller coasters, he came on in the end because somehow he felt he needed to protect me in that foreign city.

Think of all the Sunday cakes he's baked over the years, and the weekday roasts I've made. Revisit the tiny apartments and wide beaches we've shared.

We were dreamers: a scientist who went into cancer research after losing his mother to breast cancer when he was nineteen and an aspiring writer who believed words could change the world. Now he wears a suit for a pharmaceutical company and I—well. In the place of those idealists are two men who resemble them, still holding on to the other who's changed so much.

In this mythologized memorial service of our relationship, we look pretty good. For more than sixteen years we've been #relationshipgoal, before it was a hashtag—hell, before there *were* hashtags. But under the immaculate surface, too much dirty water has pooled.

I've been mourning our dying relationship for years now. It's tricky business. I can't just grieve someone who's never coming back. Every time I think

I've graduated from bargaining to depression to acceptance, the old version of Hannes resurfaces for a breather and I spin another round on this whirlpool of grief, going through the hackneyed stages of mourning again and again.

Thankfully, "Hallelujah" comes to a slow end as the singer, feeling her oats, draws out the last note to a whisper. There might as well be a single tear rolling down her face. We applaud politely.

11:15 p.m.

"Sir," says a man, landing his heavy hand on my shoulder. "You can't go."

A square-jawed Eastern European with the build of a bouncer steps up a few stairs to tower over me.

"I just need my medication," I say. "Can I go to my room? I'd hate to bother anyone."

I don't actually need anything. I'm just restless. There's only so much eavesdropping I can do to keep myself amused. I'll bring back my copy of *Moby-Dick*, the book I bring on long trips, determined to finish yet never managing to read more than a few pages.

"The stair is closed," he says.

I thought I was being sneaky, but he must have been watching the stairs from across the room. He looks exhausted, and probably also tired of nosy passengers like me.

"We bring you what you need," he says.

"Oh, my pills are impossible to find," I lie.

"It's not safe," he says.

"I can sign a waiver if I need to," I say. "I really am going to be okay."

Sitting around is making me morose. I don't want to circle the atrium over and over, looking at the same passengers.

The man eyes my sturdy boots, really not unlike a bouncer deciding if a guy's kicks are good enough for the club. "Okay, write down your cabin number. Someone will come with you."

With my newly assigned minder, a woman half my height, I retrace the steps I took nine hours ago. Nothing seems out of the ordinary under the pleasant track lighting. But like the men's room and its dirty water, there must be defects under the perfect surface.

Once I turn onto the hallway on my floor, I find a place transformed. The narrow corridor is crammed with men in tattered T-shirts and tight, faded jeans, piled into clusters and sleeping or playing games on their phones. These are not the cheery staff trained in small talk and wide smiles; these are workers who were never meant to be seen by passengers, those who toil in the bowels of the vessel operating machineries heavy and light, laundering, greasing, hammering.

All week, this hallway was a transient place, passengers politely excusing themselves as they passed one another sideways, or waiters scurrying with room ser-vice carts. Housekeeping staff materialized when most passengers were away on shore excursions or for meals and disappeared just as quickly. And when they ran into passengers, they would smile as if elated. Those crew, trained in saccharine North American customer service, are downstairs now, tending to the guests.

The corridor glows harshly. Many of the men are covering their eyes with T-shirts and whatever pieces of clothing they have on hand. Is this the real reason passengers aren't allowed back, in order to continue keeping these behind-the-scenes staff out of sight?

Strange that these men stay in packs, their limbs and torsos touching even though much of the hall-way remains empty. The air is unpleasantly warm and brimming with body odors, so it can't be for heat. Is it because they're more accustomed to existing in close quarters, having spent months crammed on top of one another? Or maybe they've been ordered to stay in clusters, as we passengers are, so they're easy to account for. Or maybe they find comfort in one another: the intimate proximity a reminder that we're not alone at sea.

The reclining men are anything but deferen-tial—a refreshing change. I tiptoe around and over them, and they don't look up or budge an inch. As far as they're concerned, I don't exist.

"Sir, please be fast and careful," says my escort, showing me to my room.

On the doorknob, a red sign hangs: EVACUATED.

Wishful thinking. I don't even want to entertain an alternate timeline.

Then again, what if some enterprising man—one of the men who had been lying in this corridor, perhaps—slipped into my room, pulled on my clothes, and seized the opportunity to hop into the helicopter? If the ship does go down, will this talented Mr. Ripley live the rest of my life for me? The thought is so unsettling and thrilling that I have to scan the hallway one more time, looking for a passable enough doppelgänger.

I want to wave my arms and shout that I, too, am working. But that's not completely honest. Being embedded on a luxury cruise ship as a travel writer is a strange in-between position. In my head, I know I don't belong with the other passengers. I don't belong with the crew, either. I've loved my cabin with a balcony; I've been indulging in the nonstop bacchanalia I didn't pay for. Most of all, I have a shot at getting airlifted long before the crew.

What I'm trying to say is that it's easier to imagine being generous when my privilege remains untouched. I want to yell *Just walk right in. Every room is empty! Enjoy the ergonomic mattresses! Raid the minibars!* but know that if I were still allowed to be in my own cabin, I would not be opening the door for strangers.

Stepping out of the bright hallway, I see another reason why nobody would want to be in the cabins. Mine looks like a hotel room trashed by a rock star battling meth-induced psychosis. Broken bits of wood and glass stick out from the carpet between upside-down furniture. The unhinged closet door slides back and forth with the rhythm of the ship; the drawers have vomited their contents.

Still, the quiet gloom inside the four walls is a welcome change. The sky is black, as is the sea, so the balcony door is just a dark mirror. I have to fight the urge to sink into the bed.

My minder clears her throat through the door left ajar. Among the debris, I pick out that copy of *Moby-Dick*.

When you're too anxious to sleep, read *Moby-Dick*. Flip open to one of the relentless chapters on cetology. Learn about the classification of this diverse species and their many, many variations, from finback to razorback to humpback. Appreciate the most minute variations in anatomy and temper. See how many pages you last before sleep claims you.

Read Melville praise whale sperm for its cosmetic qualities—not to mention its alleged virtue of disarming rage. Watch an assembly line of men extract the sperm: "Squeeze! Squeeze! Squeeze! all the morning long; I squeezed that sperm till I myself almost melted into it; I squeezed that sperm till a strange sort of insanity came over me . . ."

Moby-Dick is the Russian roulette of literature: You never know if you're about to get suspense, biology, poetry, or, maybe for niche readers, erotica. And don't you forget: The book also features what might be the first gay wedding in the Western canon.

Then there's an entire chapter dedicated to the color white, which gives us a nineteenth-century info dump by invoking every little tidbit of trivia from Greek mythology to Zoroastrianism, the "joyful" white stones in ancient Rome to the "higher horror" of whitewashed ruins in Lima. It's the queerest of intellectual flex.

Hold on tight as Melville takes a wild turn: "Or is it, that as in essence whiteness is not so much a color as the visible absence of color; and at the same time the concrete of all colors; is it for these reasons that there is such a dumb blankness, full of meaning, in a wide landscape of snows—a colorless, all-color of atheism from which we shrink?"

Viking—like every other cruise line—is obsessed with keeping its vessels as white as possible. There's a practical reason: Because the color reflects light, blanketing all exteriors in white paint keeps the ships cool.

For Melville, the color we've come to associate with cleanliness is much more complex than purity, imbued with a terror of the void. And this aggressive insistence on inoffensive blankness, I see, is one of the most terrifying things about a cruise, too: When you create a space that everyone can tolerate, you end up draining all life from it.

Then again, Melville did sneak in "This pre-eminence in [the color white] applies to the human race itself, giving the white man ideal mastership over every dusky tribe" in that very chapter. He was observing the worldview of his time, though I fear not much has changed since. I'd have to be willfully blind not to notice the supremacy—or pre-eminence, as Melville called it—of whiteness where the passenger-crew line is sharply drawn. Did I not just tiptoe through piles of workers huddled in the hallway, all of them from south of the equator? Am I not an imposter among the pale-skinned passengers?

11:55 p.m.

Fatigue has settled in around the atrium; passengers slump together, unmoving. It has been close to ten hours since we were told to gather in our muster stations. I look around for a sheltered spot and find a tall, marble-topped table. It's next to a bar where happy-hour revelers would lean as they sipped prosecco and gobbled down hors d'oeuvres. The slender piece of furniture appears to be bolted to the floor, and is just long enough that I can shrimp my tall frame in between the solid legs; the tabletop juts out just enough to shield one eye from the harsh light.

The ship continues to roll. Why do we demand to be bounced to sleep as infants, then find the same motion so unsettling when we're grown up? I sleep fitfully only to be startled awake by a dream about Hannes, though it evaporates so quickly that I can't recall a single detail. Rubbing my eyes, I sit up.

Just then, a wave broadsides us like a semi truck crashing into a bicycle. Furniture topples and slides like bowling pins. Was that a champagne bottle whooshing through the air like an arrow? Right in front of me, a couple sitting side by side and holding hands fall backward, slamming their heads so hard against the floor that I practically feel the thump. They are too stunned to move. Their heads are inches away from the marble floor and have, by some dumb luck, landed instead on thick carpet.

Everyone crouches and covers, like in an earthquake drill. A few feet behind me, computers somersault off a desk, pulling with them a dozen mobile phones that have been leeching power off their USB ports. When the shaking slows, I crawl away from the heavy table, which seemed like a refuge when I was under it but feels more like a liability now.

Funny how we bargain with fate. When we were near the shore, those water-sharpened rocks seemed like death traps. Now, having sailed for hours away from land, I wish we were back near the coast, almost convinced I could swim to safety.

The bar has exploded. Drawers open and close, revealing rattling cans inside. On the floor, decapitated bottles drown in a mixed pool of alcohol. A fridge flaps its door, which doesn't seem to fit anymore. The register's monitor has managed to stay on and receipts with drink orders curl out from its small black printer.

Next to the bar, half a chair has broken through a door to an office that I'd never noticed before. The door's shiny metal frame is bent outward, and the milky glass looks like the melting surface of a frozen lake, oddly beautiful.

It's only when I stand and try to walk up the wide stairs to the upper level of the atrium that it becomes clear how much the ship is listing. As if drunk, I cross the entire width diagonally in a halting stagger, the ground beneath my feet angling left and right.

The captain comes back on the PA and says the ship is "fairly under control."

Polynesians sailed thousands of miles to settle a constellation of islands across the Pacific. Arab seafarers consulted magnetic compasses to bypass mountain ranges and deserts in order to conquer lands from the Mediterranean to the Indian Ocean. In the tenth century, Norse explorers went to Newfoundland in search of timber and fish before learning the hard way that, oops, there were already folks—with arrows—who were none too happy about their intrusion.

After playing a feature role in human history, ships could have become obsolete. Airplanes overtook ocean liners as the preferred mode of crossing the Atlantic in the mid-twentieth century. Enter leisure cruises. These floating palaces were already in existence, after all, and they had to be put to some use. In many ways, cruises have always been steeped in nostalgia for the era that immediately preceded them. From the beginning, these unnecessary vessels mournfully harked to a bygone age. And is there anything more universal than nostalgia and mourning?

Given humans' helplessness in aquatic environments, it may not come as a surprise that cruises are rife with incidents of all shades. In 2010, the *Celebrity Mercury* saw a norovirus outbreak so rapid that 413 passengers were stricken and the ship turned into a veritable vomitorium. In 2013, a generator fire aboard the *Carnival Triumph*, on the other hand, left that ship without power for five days, stranding the passengers and crew to float aimlessly without plumbing. Late-night talk-show hosts were only too happy to nickname the ship the "Carnival Toilet" and the "Poop Cruise"—so it's no wonder that Carnival Corporation quietly changed the ship's name to the less triumphant *Sunrise*.

Fan sites like Cruise Junkie and Cruise Mapper gleefully list accidents ranging from catastrophic engine failures to ships running aground. It's a wonder that those enthusiasts would go aboard in the first place—or why cruises should exist at all, for that matter. Nostalgia must be one hell of a demon if it makes us overlook cruises' pitfalls, not to mention the wake of pollution they leave behind. Are we all trying to outrun our collective grief about the passage of time? Are cruises the ultimate escape from our on-the-ground present tense?

Cruises reflect modern travel at its most blatant. The word *travel* shares the root of the French word *travailler*: to work. *Travail* means strenuous labor. In Middle English, *travelen* meant "to torment." One theory connects the word to *tripalium*, an ancient Roman method of torture involving impaling with three stakes. We've sure come a long way to think of travel as fun.

Today's passengers drown in a pampering we feel we've earned. We might even throw around words like *sybaritic*. And lest you accuse me of hypocrisy, let me be the first to cast the stone and admit that I have made a living as a professional tourist who's used the word *sybaritic* once or a dozen times in my magazine career.

From a cruise ship, we passengers with the correctly colored passports get to waddle down the gangway to the concrete pier, where hired locals greet us with folk dancing and shower us with flower petals. At the end of the day, we return to our bubble, ready to float across the very national borders we've built to keep many people exactly where they are.

The whole sleek façade of cruises is built upon the travails of workers. The employees, in turn, keep up their own code of hierarchy that waterfalls from Mediterranean officers in uniforms and Eastern European department heads. Fair-skinned entertainers stand before the Filipino musicians who are relegated to the back. And housekeeping staff who are conversant in English collect tips that may never get trickled down to the launderers tucked deep inside the ship's bowels: It's a "Small World After All" of horrors.

Then again, don't the workers sign up knowing exactly what they're getting into? Don't the remittances they send home pay rent, send kids to school, build houses, change lives? Aren't the bright young staff broadening their horizons while seeing the world, meeting people around the globe, learning life lessons? Aren't many of them doing exactly what I try to do?

Travel really does change us. It's changed me. It's been the best private education I've received. And like many other backpackers, I could do so on a shoestring because of the price our parents paid in advance, in the currency of education and encouragement. To refute this privilege—the very privilege my parents worked so hard to grant me—would be the ultimate act of privilege.

The cruise industry didn't create the disparity; it's merely holding up a mirror. And if it makes me uneasy, it's because I am aware that I prefer not to dwell on the widening distance between upstairs and downstairs.

Besides, looking away in denial has become my second nature. I've gotten real good at ignoring the obvious.

Take it from me. If you want the security of a long-term relationship and the thrill of cheating at the same time, find yourself a travel-writer boyfriend.

I knew Hannes was having sex with other men when I was out of town for days and weeks at a time. I came to the realization slowly. Perhaps I was too naïve; maybe I was just being what I was supposed to be in a relationship: trusting. I figured things out only once Hannes could no longer limit his cheating to the days when I was on assignment. All-nighters "at the lab," ATM receipts from odd parts of the city, a stranger's underwear in our hamper. A call in the middle of dinner that he claims is from his father, who lives in Germany where it's four o'clock in the morning. Canceled plans, forgotten birthdays, missed anniversaries. The more absurd the alibis became, the harder I tried to ignore what was happening; eventually I stopped asking.

Why do I stick around despite such humiliation? Where's my pride?

When I'm away—on assignment like this, for example—I know breaking up is the only right thing to do. But when I return home and see Hannes, I lose all resolve. We've long lost our attraction to each other, yet this is the sleight of hand humans have named love, this queer mix of muscle memory and personal history that binds two people together, sometimes despite their best efforts. If we do fall asleep together, we wake up perfectly fitted like two question marks.

Besides, breaking up is scary when you've never known adult life without each other. It would also mean divvying up years of memories. Fear freezes me up. It's easier to let inertia carry me deeper into the storm while I wish for a rescuer to drop from the sky and winch me away.

If I have any pride left, I reserve it to keep up appearance and maintain a respectable upstairs so our relationship can stay afloat. I can't tell friends— they'd lose any respect they have for me. I can't tell my parents, who'd nod silently, knowingly, then break into passionate speeches about how they've never liked him anyway. I can't let down my preteen nieces, who've known me all their lives as nothing other than one half of their favorite uncle pair. The visible part of us is beautiful—so who cares about all the injuries piling up below sea level? The only thing left in my control is deciding what I keep out of sight.

Many couples I know have told me—openly, if they're gay, and in hushed voices if they're straight— how it saved their unions to open up their relationships and sleep with other people. Eventually, Hannes and I settled on calling our arrangement an open relationship. We didn't crack a joke about being *mal-baisé*.

To save face, I told my friends that I was having a Rumspringa, appropriating the Amish rite of passage when youth shed the strict rules of their faith and run free for a short time. I did feel as if I was thrust suddenly into the present after living years in an obsolete life. I'd gone into my make-believe bubble with Hannes long before the GPS-powered hookup apps and one-pill-a-day HIV prevention. Bewildered by the new world I found awaiting me in my rumspringa, I relied on my friend Jacques, who appointed himself my fairy godmother—or simply "mama," as he took to calling himself—to help me decipher love in the time of PrEP. He ghostwrote my dating profiles and tried in vain to get me to show some skin. Despite his clever one-liners meant to get me laid with no strings attached, I often attracted the kind of guys who wanted to take me home to meet their moms—this was, Jacques lamented, because of my Big Martha Stewart Energy.

My friend Weber once said men have no choice but to look outside when they don't get what they want at home. I hated myself for the ways in which I must have failed the relationship and forced Hannes to look elsewhere. Then, when I learned the sheer scale of Hannes's lies, I felt strangely relieved: As he slowly admitted—in excruciating phases—to having slept with hundreds of men before we'd even officially opened up the relationship, I realized he had been looking for something that couldn't be found in any home, let alone ours.

Now, eyes bleary after an exhausting night, I glance at my phone. Hannes and I haven't called each other in hours.

4:45 a.m.

The P.A. system crackles. The captain sounds hoarse.

"Nothing's new," he says. "As soon as we get daylight, we'll do our best."

We have been drifting farther and farther out to sea: safer than running aground, but leaving us at the ocean's whim. As the portholes turn from black to the faint gray of dawn, we see how angry the sea remains. My throat feels sandy; I slept barely an hour.

Remarkably, none of my friends—as connected to the internet as they are—has placed me in the sensational news item of a cruise ship adrift. Over the past few hours, I've been texting a few friends who randomly pop into mind, writing something along the lines of "I don't think we say 'I love you' enough" and "Just want you to know I'm thinking of you."

Hours after my cryptic not-saying-goodbye-but-kind-of-saying-goodbye message, Jacques writes back:

"Are you having a Rose moment on your cruise?" he texts, referencing Kate Winslet and Leonardo DiCaprio in *Titanic*. "You jump, I jump!" Along with his message, he's sent a GIF of the movie's most meme-ready scene of the two young lovers at the bow of the ship, flying, cheesy to the core. Maybe it's the exhaustion, but I laugh, deliriously.

The normalcy of interactions like these calms me—there's no drama, just affectionate teasing between friends. No one I text seems to have seen the news. At least I hope that's the case; otherwise I need to find kinder friends who might actually mourn me when I'm gone.

Cheryl is annoyed: "Why are you texting me? Aren't you supposed to be on some fancy boat?"

"You're one of my executors," I text back. "Remember, everything I own goes to my parents."

"You're freaking me out," she responds. "Are you okay?"

This is my chance to tell her I'm not okay, that I haven't been for years.

"I'm fine," I write. "Just being an anxious insomniac. Sorry I worried you."

Everything I own. Sounds so grandiose. But I do mean it: Inheritance of every kind—money, heirloom objects, family lore—belongs to my family, not Hannes.

Seventy-some Years Ago

Sometime around 1948, my father, aged six or seven, was in the midst of his own maritime disaster in the making. He was somewhere in the small but unpredictable pocket of the Pacific Ocean between Korea and Japan. He was heading to the homeland he'd never seen.

At the end of WWII, my family was among the 2.4 million ethnic Koreans living in Japan. Some were bright-eyed university students, some enthusiastic colonial collaborators, others laborers conscripted during the three decades of Japanese occupation of Korea.

The Kwaks were none of the above. My grandparents had taken the gamble of moving across the strait in search of a better life. They settled in Takarazuka, a sleepy foothill town nuzzled between Osaka and Kobe, unremarkable in every way except for its famous traditional troupe of male-impersonating actresses.

My grandparents opened a hardware shop and did well for themselves, well enough to have oranges in their pantry during the height of wartime shortages. One of the few fragments of memory my father carried from his foreign birthplace is the neighbors coming by time and again to borrow refined sugar, an indulgence back then—a proud memory, perhaps, for this family of immigrants.

A couple of years after Korea's independence, in 1945, the Kwaks joined their compatriots in moving homeward, crossing the sea that, at its narrowest, would barely take a day to navigate. But they didn't have what we take for granted now: pinpoint navigation, by-the-minute weather forecasts, rescue helicopters. Nothing was certain. In a world that had become more entangled through wars, journeys had grown shorter but no less perilous.

Take, for example: the *Gonron Maru*. In 1943, the six-month-old, 7,900-ton ship was sailing to Korea when the American submarine USS *Wahoo* discharged torpedoes. The U.S. Navy was acting on intelligence that there were 2,000 Japanese soldiers on board. But life being as random as it is, a derailed train had stranded those soldiers on land in Japan. The steamer left anyway, carrying only civilians: traders, migrants, homebound students. More than 580 would perish.

The end of the war didn't guarantee safety, either. The *Ukishima Maru*, an auxiliary warship, left a Japanese military base in Aomori, at the northern tip of the main island of Honshu, one week after the Japanese emperor surrendered. On board were more than 4,000 Koreans, 3,725 of whom were forced laborers, at last free to return home, and their families. Two days into the voyage, a little more than halfway through the journey, the ship made a resupplying pit stop in the port of Maizaru, near Kyoto. Pulling away from port for the final leg, the ship struck a magnetic mine. More than 500 passengers drowned just off the shore of their captors' land. Those on board were not the people whom history books honor—just bit players on the chaotic stage that had seen too many anonymous casualties already.

I'd never heard of either of these ships or their tragic ends until I began digging around for my own family's history.

So, it's no surprise that I can't find any historical record of my father's homeward voyage. And can you blame him, then just a child, for not remembering much of the trip, let alone the exact date? My grandparents are gone, and Dad's older siblings can't recall the name of their ship, either. Perhaps they've all willed themselves into burying the memory. Whatever records they may have had—boarding passes, entry documents—were lost to time. But when I look at the map of Japan, it sends chills down my spine to see that you can draw a straight line north from Takarazuka, where my family lived, to the port of Maizaru, where the mine explosion drowned hundreds of my compatriots. It's very possible that my father also left Japan from Maizaru—a different day, a different fate.

Had the *Ukishima Maru*'s course out of Maizaru veered just a few feet differently in 1945—and that's a big *if*, because some scholars and the victims' descendants believe the explosion was no accident—and had the underwater mine lain dormant and undetected for just a couple of years longer, could the ship carrying my family have been the one happening upon it?

No matter how hard we try to make up narratives to explain past events, history seems to me no more logical than it is compassionate. No, my family's story unfolded this way: What should have been a quick journey instead stretched on for days as the ship lost its bearings in bad weather and kept drifting down toward the South China Sea—nothing silky about it.

This part gets hazy. The version my dad tells has the ship end up all the way to the Gulf of Tonkin, which seems an impossibly faraway distance to go while lost. As the ship ran out of provisions, my grandfather sought out the captain, who had eyed his wristwatch.

When my father insists that it was an extravagant Patek Philippe watch on my grandfather's wrist, my inner skeptic takes me on a wild internet goose chase. Were there luxury Swiss watches in Japan at the time? During my grandparents' immigrant years, building a business must not have been easy. A Korean in Japan was a second-class citizen, no matter how perfectly he spoke Japanese. (The Imperial Japanese government banned the native language in schools in Korea, which meant any educated person would read and write and curse in the language of the colonizers.) Despite the fluency in Japanese, could an ordinary immigrant have done well enough for himself to afford a hand-made European watch?

Then again, embarking on an uncertain home-bound journey in that era, long before travel insurance became readily available, wouldn't you opt for the safest, most compact form of currency to carry on you? And if my father is a reflection of his own father, then I believe in a heartbeat that this man I never met would have always bought the best in class of everything. Besides, if you're leaving a land that has always regarded you as less than equal, who wouldn't want to wear some crazy, ostentatious bling?

My grandparents, who'd worked to make certain their children would want for nothing even at the height of WWII, weren't about to let them go hungry. So, my father's version of the story goes, my grandfather found the master of the ship and traded his prized wristwatch for the last grains of rice on board. Who cares whether it was a Patek Philippe? Let it be a factory-made Timex shaped like Mickey Mouse for all I care. The point is this: My grandfather, a man who would die decades before I was born, gave away what was dear to him so that his family could live.

Days later, exhausted but not starved, my family landed in Gunsan, on the opposite side of the Korean peninsula from their original destination. My father's first sight of his homeland was of a place his family had never been.

Why am I—sleep-deprived, thirsty, wistful, listing side to side on a moaning cruise ship—thinking about a secondhand past? Maybe it's because there's no point speculating when your future seems not only uncertain, but also random. I have no way of knowing what will happen in the next minute much less in an hour, but at least there are some truths upon which I can plant my feet. I suppose this is what faith means to some; for me, knowing where I come from is my gravity.

7:45 a.m.

Fifteen hours. That's how long the tugboat *Vivax* has been at the *Viking Sky*'s side. In this storm, the crew of four can't even boil a pot of coffee.

A ribbon of sunlight floats in from the horizon. The waves have quieted by half, down from twenty or thirty feet to ten or fifteen. Leif Arne Sørenes, the master of the tugboat, senses that a window of opportunity has opened.

Instead of risking the messenger line losing its way and getting into the cruise ship's propeller, the *Vivax* approaches the cruise ship's aft. There, a *Viking Sky* seaman has positioned himself in the lower hatch. As in Michelangelo's *The Creation of Adam* in the Sistine Chapel, the tugboat's able seaman reaches up, not with a finger but with the tug line, stretching toward the Filipino sailor leaning as far out of the *Viking Sky* as he can.

8:10 a.m.

"Ladies and gentlemen," the captain announces. "We have successfully connected to a tugboat."

A ripple of cheers breaks the surface tension of

the atrium's silence. It feels as if I'm in the audience of a TV game show where I don't understand the game or the prize, but I still get swept up and applaud with others.

"Bad news is, we have to turn around," the captain continues. "There will be some roll. We will do our best."

We can't completely grasp what the captain has just told us, but after more than eighteen hours since the engines failed, we finally have a purpose. Eyes bleary and legs cramped, we spring up. The atrium has the same bustle as a campground morning. As the ship fills with commotion, the crew enlist us to help move furniture. While we cheerily help, the seriousness of what's coming next begins to sink in. With two tugboats acting like poles, we will be spun 180 degrees, exposing our sides to the pounding waves. When I realize that the ship could be broadsided again, it brings back the nauseating sensation of tipping toward the sea.

We have developed a different relationship to windows. Until yesterday, we flocked to the glass portals, leaned against them, and gazed outside wistfully to admire the mountains and glaciers. That was before the sea breached through and doused some of us in freezing water. Now, we fear the windows.

We push all the furniture away from the walls and stack it, Jenga-like, in the middle of the room, hoping it won't all topple and fly against the windows. Once there seems to be nothing left to do on the upper level, I head down to the base of the atrium and repeat:

Carry, stack, carry, stack. I can't guarantee I'm helping, but at least I'm doing something.

The last of the helicopters has left, the captain announces. Everyone still on board is in it together now. "It might be some heavy rolling," he says. "I hope not. But the likelihood is high. Please, once again, sit down."

Maybe the library—or the corner of the atrium that used to be the library, anyway—isn't the smartest choice for a bunker, but that's where I happen to be when the captain orders us to stay in place. The books that didn't already fall off the shelves have been stacked into short piles on the floor to prevent them from scattering. I scan the spines as a I look for a place to plop down.

Can it be . . .?

Among the library's haphazard collection of hardcovers, I spot a coffee-table topper I know all too well: a photographic anthology, one of those "destinations of a lifetime" type of books that *National Geographic* puts out each Christmas to supplement its flagging magazine sales. Weighing as much as a dumbbell, the book brims with glossy, alluring photographs—and purple prose, some of which I produced.

It's jarring to encounter this book in the wild. Once it was published, I regifted all of my contributor's copies and never thought about the project again. I'm pretty sure they are gathering dust under my relatives' glass-topped coffee tables, opened for a brief few seconds by their friends before coffee is served. And if those visitors glanced at my over-the-top odes to far-away destinations—and that's a big "if" because these books really exist for the photographs—then I take solace in the fact that my name wasn't attached to any of the essays written in superlatives.

Oh.

I *have* written books. I've written travel guides, contributed to anthologies, and, if you count ghostwriting, even completed two books on architecture. So why do I keep whining that I've never accomplished what I really want? Staring at the coffee-table book—one of many I've written for—I realize that publishing a book isn't actually my dream, never has been. It's just been a name I gave to a longing I may never fulfill.

I'm not proud of many of my bylines. I've come to prefer *not* attaching my name to projects like this coffee-table book—because then I can assure myself that I did it just for the paycheck. I don't have to try hard; I can shrug and move on to the next job.

I've long stopped feeling heartbroken when an editor removes a memorable interview subject from an article or rewrites an entire scene. Call it growing up; call it getting real. But it's come at a great cost. I began to see writing as merely something I could price by the word. That may have been when I stopped aspiring.

What I really want isn't to simply write books and have them published. It's to dream again. To believe in the written word and not merely add to the cacophony of noise overflowing our digital world. To hold something and not be ashamed to admit I gave my all to it. To hope I've created something that's better than I am. For so long, it's been easier to be flippant than to wear my heart on my sleeve.

Have I been too afraid of heartbreak to actually live? And has that fear colored every choice I've made?

Instead of risking all, I've chosen the dull, daily ache of dwelling inside the make-believe space Hannes and I carved out for ourselves years ago. And though I've known for a long time that everything is falling apart underneath, I've kept up the pretense that nothing's amiss.

In the grand scheme of things, one lost day is just a blink of an eye. But when you suspect the ship you're on may soon sink, every minute stretches. And when you know for sure you're drifting away from the direction you intended, every second is excruciating. Maybe my real problem is that there's never been a catastrophic engine failure in my life. Instead, I've been drifting slowly and steadily off course, acting out a job that I no longer enjoy, blaming my shortcomings on the editors, and staying in a relationship that my partner and I have both outgrown—while lying, all in the name of sparing my loved ones the pain of my truth.

"The U-turn is complete," the captain announces.

The passengers look at one another, bewildered. We were so disoriented that we didn't even notice the ship turning. The same sea that threatened to pull us down for hours simply licked the ship's sides like a puppy as the tugboats led us in a smooth ball-room-style half circle.

Now, a new direction—which is really the old way. For us to start anew on dry land, we must retrace the very route we've just sailed.

When Captain Gustafsson walks through the atrium for a victory lap moments after the U-turn, passengers throw themselves in his path to pump his hand with hardy handshakes.

"It's so wonderful to be under your care," says one woman, just about ready to kiss his ring. "Thank you, thank you, thank you."

Listening to the captain's disembodied voice, I pictured a cross between growling Ahab and a beleaguered Tom Hanks from that modern-day pirate movie; in reality, the master of our ship looks nothing like either. As Captain Gustafsson walks by, he seems too—for the lack of a better word—*nice.* He is mild-mannered, ordinary even. I wouldn't throw a second glance his way if I passed him on a street. How does it feel to be responsible for not one but 1,373 lives? And when he's on land, shopping for groceries or taking out the trash, how does it feel *not* to be important?

I hear a faint Muzak rendition of "Edelweiss" piping through the same speakers that were, until moments ago, relaying only the captain's assurances. Nearby, there's a spirited game of Yahtzee starting up.

"Come on, you're still on a cruise," shouts a crew member, weaving in and out of the crowd. "You gotta overeat!"

Downstairs, massive foil trays appear, steamy with shrimp stew, pork cutlet, and French fries. There's even a giant bowl brimming with a thoroughly tossed Caesar salad. This is not a haphazard buffet of whatever's left, but rather a planned meal as solid as the nutritional pyramid. How on earth did they whip up this feast for a thousand people after the day we've had?

This may be the only time the crew and passengers line up together for food. We're all here: the passengers mingling with those who smile and perform for us and those trained to be invisible. Before the heaping portions of salad and stew, the two worlds merge—albeit for the briefest moment—into a single strange family, bonded.

As the captain continues his goodwill tour, the cleaners, the below-deck crew, and kitchen staff pile food onto their paper plates. Then they disappear again.

2:05 p.m.

It's been twenty-four hours since Mayday. When we're finally allowed to return to our cabins, I practically dash, leaping two, three steps at a time.

Throwing open my cabin door, I'm stunned. My room has that look of a freshly made-up hotel suite. The bed is not only reassembled but also fitted with crisp sheets folded in tidy hospital corners. On the bureau, sparkling tumblers replace the ones the storm smashed against the wall. I can't begin to grasp what the crew must have gone through—fear and fatigue aside—to fix and tidy hundreds of rooms back to their original shape. The closet door doesn't slide unhinged: Every screw has been tightened, each little wheel forced back into the track. Most eerie of all, the TV set is tuned to the same movie I was watching before the power went out, cued to exactly where we left off. Mary, please, as if I could plop back onto the bed and resume watching *Mary, Queen of Scots*.

But I don't want to pretend the last twenty-four hours never happened. They can rewind every clock on the ship and try to convince me that we get to do yesterday over. Underneath the shiny surface everything has changed.

I peel off all the layers of clothing—parka, sweater, merino undershirt. My stench startles me. I lift an arm and sniff. Is this what they mean by smelling fear? Thanks to a common genetic mutation that my people carry, I can sweat for hours and my wet, transparent shirt will still smell like laundry detergent. Now, I'm equal parts wet dog, vinegar, and rotting fruit. It cracks me up—I am a broken machine, unable to stop grimacing and making a noise that sounds like laughter and looks like laughter in the mirror but sure doesn't feel like laughter. My very existence both fascinates and repulses me. I wish I could shed my skin, and at the same time I wish I could curl up and fester in my own stink.

The shower only sputters brown water. I resort to the cruise version of a birdbath: wet wipes, rubbed down from head to toe. Afterwards I head out to meet Peter, the photographer, as we'd planned earlier. By now we're all but sure that both our assignments are goners. Cruise companies are some of the largest ad buyers in the travel publications that pay our rent; glossy magazines can't cut those purse strings by covering an accident. Still, we can't help ourselves. We put on our freelancer hats and snoop around.

The Explorers Lounge, where we sat among septuagenarians for a trivia quiz yesterday, looks like a doll's house dropped from a third-floor balcony. The baby grand piano is flipped upside down in the middle of a herd of plush armchairs. Planter boxes have been scattered about and vomited soil all across the carpet.

"Check this out," Peter says, leading me to the middle of the mezzanine. A heavy vitrine case has face-planted and shattered, yet its sole occupant—a delicate model ship—is immaculate, firmly attached to its base and hovering just a few inches above thick chunks of glass.

The curved stairway still floats elegantly, but the glass panel running alongside the handrail has cracked into thousands of pieces and threatens to crumble at the slightest touch. Ceiling panels have crashed down, yet a giant globe on a pedestal stands proudly. I turn and turn the orb, letting my finger graze its shiny, unmarred surface.

A spiderweb of cracks spreads from a hole on one of the exterior window panes. How many other holes are there? How many can't we see?

Peter clicks away with his heavy camera. There's something clinical and dispassionate about the way he's capturing the images, like a coroner studying a body. Every now and then, he betrays his impassive façade and mutters "Wow . . ."

We're past simply recording. We've become scalpel-happy participants in this autopsy. The shabby layer just beneath the luxurious skin endears the ship to me: Small side tables have broken, revealing their legs to be flimsy compressed wood merely glued to the tabletops. I'm ashamed to entertain the thought but I can't help it: Will the next few hours give us the real scoop that will pay our bills?

We amble up to the indoor pool, which has been drained and is filled with dozens of deck chairs and chaise lounges that have fallen in. It looks like an art installation about the fragile excess of cruises. We head back downstairs. I've walked up and down many, many times over the past week, but standing on these cushy steps while waiting to evacuate yesterday was the only time I ever lingered here. Now it feels uncouth to just pass, as if I'm rushing through every room in a museum of ethnography.

Then again, without all those scared and hopeful people, this is just a staircase, nothing more.

In the restaurant, Peter and I stand over the many-layered metal door, now lying on the floor and crumpled like a piece of aluminum foil. The border between what could have been and what ended up being was in constant change yesterday. Now that I think about it, though, isn't that always the case? We get to live but one random path that exists out of many possible permutations. Our timeline rolls down this one-way slope, denying us of all the could-haves and would-haves splintering off from the main path. When we look back, we may try to assign meaning to every little turn, twist, and bump to make up an inevitable plot. But there's no such thing as destiny. Life just happened so. And though we may get glimpses of a few things that never took place, we don't get to pick another path, like cheating in a Choose Your Own Adventure book. Maybe that's what makes it so jarring to be confronted with sights like this crushed door, an unopened portal to an alternate fate.

Think about it: We start as microscopic strands of genetic materials that beat near-impossible odds to become life. After nine months of parasitic existence, we continue living helplessly for years while we're fed, wiped, and prevented from sticking a finger into an electric socket until we're reasonably self-sufficient. Zoom out a little more and you find that we exist by the grace of dumb luck, standing on a brittle crust wrapped around a pressurized cauldron of molten slush, flying through an icy vacuum that stretches to infinity. That our blue marble happens to tilt just so, at exactly the right distance from the sun, to sustain a thin film of breathable air is a wonder of physics.

To speak of luck is perhaps the most mundane and fundamental aspect of human existence: Our very being is serendipitous.

In order for us passengers to stay safe, hundreds of workers and volunteers stayed up through the night and gave their all. Yet just one tiny difference beyond anyone's control—a current that pushed us a little too hard, say, or an underwater boulder that had been a little closer—could have easily tipped us into the watery void. Surviving such an obvious near disaster makes me wonder about all the close calls I've likely dodged over the years—the same coincidences that make me grateful to be alive, but can also paralyze me in fear if I dwell on such thoughts for too long.

In the ship's basement, the fitness center is a cubist sketch: sixty-pound dumbbells carelessly flung around and treadmills meeting one another at jagged angles. In the duty-free shop next door, Dior handbags and compact cases blanket the floor like a department store heist gone really, really wrong. But those dainty sample bottles of perfume? Still sparkling and secured to the walls.

My grandmother—the same woman who knew the terror of the almost-but-not-quite-disastrous journey from Japan to Korea, she of the no-soup-be-fore-travel fame—used to say that water is the scariest force of all.

"At least fire will leave ash," she would say. "Water will erase everything without a trace."

Actually, it turns out she inherited this nugget of insight from her mother-in-law, my great-grandmother. And I'll pass it on, too, adding my own spin: Water may erase everything without a trace, but it also spares the most random and undeserving among us, like duty-free perfume samples.

It can also spare people who are grateful for a second chance, like me.

3:50 p.m.

The tugboats pull us into a sheltered fjord. We glide on flat water. The sparse mountainscape gives way to apartment buildings and homes. Thumping Eurotrash beats blast from balconies, where onlookers are jumping up and down, waving the national flag.

Did Norway just pulverize Sweden in a soccer match? Oh.

They're celebrating that we're alive.

With whoops and claps, the people of Molde are cheering for the 894 of us—436 passengers and 458 crew members—who remain on the ship. Strollers on the waterfront join in welcoming what might be the most famous ship to pull into this city of 27,000.

Passengers lean out from their balconies, waving as if they're visiting monarchs and taking pictures with their iPads.

"We love you, Norway!" shouts my neighbor from her balcony. "God bless you, Norway!"

Television crews from British and Norwegian news outlets are ready on the dock; journalists in windbreakers have taken their places in front of cameramen. On the television screen in my cabin, the BBC is showing live coverage of our arrival. From the outside, the ship looks absolutely normal.

It is well past five o'clock when local police sign off on the ship's manifest—they wouldn't want stowaways coming ashore, now would they? It's been twenty-seven hours since the ordeal began. I walk slowly down the gangplank. Most of the cameras are gone and the heroes' welcome has fizzled out.

It's just another pale evening in this small Norwegian city. All of the stores are shuttered except for a sweater shop that has opened especially for us and is doing brisk business selling woolen caps and knit cardigans. I don't want to buy anything, but I thumb through a rack of soft sweaters as I would the pages of a book. I'm moved by the sheer ordinariness—the smell of something cinnamony, a radio newscaster hushed to a low hum, the shopkeeper opening the cash register to make change for the couple who just bought up a storm.

Outside, I marvel at walking on ground that's not heaving; the cold air feels like a dessert. An icy dusk is sinking over this tidy little place. It feels like a punch in the gut to miss home so much. I don't mean the apartment I share with Hannes in San Francisco, my parents' suburban house outside Seattle, or any other place I can touch. I miss the *feeling* of home, that coziness of the heart. I haven't felt it in so long—for years.

The sun is gone. It's time to return to the ship for one final night.

Walking back toward the water, my mind wanders. Having learned the most valuable lesson of my life, I decide to dedicate the rest of my years to altruism by giving away all my possessions and moving to Shangri-La to . . .

No, that's not how this plays out.

Instead, I fire up one of those "dating" apps I've taken to using in my year of Rumspringa. I'm not only fresh meat, but also an instant celebrity, getting bombarded with more messages than usual. "Were you a crew member on the *Viking Sky*?" they want to know. "What was it like? Do you want to come over?"

I walk up a few blocks to a neat, unremarkable home on a leafy street. The man who greets me is, as most men in these situations are, older and pudgier than the pictures he'd shared on his profile. No matter. I know his full name and where he works. Jacques likes to poke fun and call it my mumsy tendency, but I can't help it; I cross-reference Facebook, Instagram, and LinkedIn before I meet up with anyone, so by the time I actually see someone in the flesh, I practically know his extended family.

I walk into the man's uncluttered living room dominated by a large flat screen.

"You were in the news all day," says the man. "Everyone in Norway was watching your ship."

A documentary about Air France flight 4590, the *Concorde* that crashed in 2000, is playing. Hasn't he had enough of real-life drama?

I'm not attracted to him, timid and a little slackened everywhere. I don't leave, either. In silence, we watch engineers talk about the supersonic aircraft that blew up.

Under normal circumstances, I might ask him what it's like to live in Molde, what it's like to be a Norwegian nonprofiteer, what he really thinks of Success Cake—playing an amateur anthropologist. Today I don't feel much like talking.

"So, what do you feel like doing?" he asks after a while.

"I . . . I want . . ."

I want a drink of water. I want a really long massage. I want to watch a horror film, the goreless kind that has Nicole Kidman running around a darkened house for two hours. More than anything else, I want one thing desperately.

"Can I use your shower?" I ask.

My poor parents—what would they say if they could see me now, having dodged yesterday's disaster, only to tempt fate again by getting naked in a stranger's bathroom? I take my sweet time scrubbing and lathering; I might even whistle. The strong, hot water makes my knees go weak. I want to lie down and fall asleep in this perfect, steam-filled glass cube.

Eventually I have to step out. I see the towel this stranger has laid out for me on the sink. It's so thick and plush that my hand almost disappears into its fabric. I hold it against my face and breathe in deep. As I exhale, tears begin to flow. To muffle my crying, I bury my face deeper into the towel. I can't stop sobbing. I have to go home, wherever that may be.

"The book's about being stuck," I hear myself say. "Actually, it's more about trying to change course when things go south. And about the randomness of fate. It feels embarrassingly melodramatic, because I get pretty confessional . . . but, god forbid, I hope the memoir doesn't sound me-moi-me-moi-me-moi. Oh, I also interview a bunch of people and write from their perspectives, which of course makes me feel like a fraud. And I guess it also touches on global inequality, too . . . but I never even get around to the pollution caused by . . ."

"That sounds great, but what is the book *about?*" asks Vanita.

"Oh. Um, it's about a cruise. We lost power off the coast of Norway."

"I remember!" says Vanita. "That's the one that almost went down, right?"

"I guess," I say. "But it wasn't a disaster."

"Then what was it?"

I have no answer.

Vanita and I are each in our apartments on opposite

coasts. At the moment, our lives look much the same: We rarely venture out from home and when we do, we shun people as if they're zombies. We no longer eat inside restaurants, sweat next to strangers in gyms, or hug our friends. Vanita walks through a nearby cemetery every day; I read the Sunday newspaper on the terrace. Otherwise, we're stuck inside. Human contact is a memory—traveling with hundreds or thousands of passengers aboard a cruise ship sounds like a relic of another era.

We are only six months into this global pandemic.

During the chaos of the quarantine's first weeks, while I scrounged for basic necessities like toilet paper and flour, the one-year anniversary of the cruise passed without my realizing it until my smartphone created an unprompted slide show entitled "For You: Memories from Norway!" In the midst of this already surreal moment, the images from just one year ago felt foreign and familiar at once, not unlike a movie that once engrossed me.

I can't serve you some neat closure. The Accident Investigation Board of Norway published an interim report that identified low lubricating oil as the reason for the debacle. When the sea tossed us, the sloshing oil failed to reach the pumps. As a result, the engines automatically shut down instead of grinding themselves to a fire. The sophisticated ocean liner's safety measures turned it into an unwieldy monument of steel and marble. The interim report ends on a cliffhanger: Why were there no fewer than eighteen low oil alarms that morning, all of them dismissed? You'll have to wait for the sequel, the final report, to find out. But I understand all too well the desire to ignore warning signs and carry on.

On these quiet nights and days of physical confinement, my mind drifts to the calamity that never was. When your radius is limited to your home, it's easy to chute down the internet rabbit hole. I'm chasing after lives that converged on a cruise ship before scattering in all directions around the globe. For hours I hunch over my laptop in San Francisco.

In Aalborg, Denmark, a man sees an unfamiliar American number flash on his cell phone. He picks up and hears me ask, "Are you Jim H. Nielsen, the helicopter pilot?"

"Yes, this is he."

I found his name from an interview that ran in the European Cockpit Association's newsletter. I spotted him on LinkedIn, which tipped me off that I had been looking in the wrong country all along: He wasn't Norwegian. He turned up three times in what I think is the Danish equivalent of the White Pages. Only one of those numbers worked.

I wanted—no, *needed*—to hear Jim's side of the story. I know the facts; I've read hundreds of articles. I need to know how he *felt*.

"Frankly, I wasn't feeling much," he says. "You think about the fuel, equipment, and not crashing."

He promises to pass my email address to his rescue man after our long phone call.

Erlend Birkeland puts his hands behind his head and leans back. Even pixeled on my computer and in the fluorescent light of the control room, which would make most people look sickly, he's the picture of health, lean and trim. Decades of cross-country skiing and scuba diving have kept him spry.

"The day after? I guess I was tired. Happy and relieved. A little proud," he says. "Above all, grateful that everything went well."

It's well past midnight where he is, a concrete platform in the North Sea. Statfjord B, an offshore base that can house two hundred in the middle of the ocean, was the heaviest man-made object ever to be moved when in 1982 it was towed out and dropped halfway between Scotland and Norway. On this temporary island, Birkeland spends most of his time waiting and reading. ("Have you read Maja Lunde?" he asks. "Oh, she wrote a fantastic novel about beekeeping. I think you'd enjoy it.") If there's a more exciting thing to do on this Friday night, say a dorm party, then he's skipping it to talk to me, a stranger halfway around the world.

Even as he matter-of-factly recounts how the rocking ship almost slammed into him on his third descent, he insists there was no drama. He's modest in the way that rescue workers are, with the I-was-just-doing-my-job self-effacement trailing every other comment like a footnote.

Weeks later, when I send him the early section of my manuscript where he makes an appearance, he corrects details. He points out things big and small—like the Sikorsky S-92 helicopter having no skids, which makes me cut out a whole scene that, frankly, read more like *Saving Private Ryan* fan fic.

So how does he feel about seeing himself painted in someone else's words?

"Reading it feels okay!" he messages back. "Strange, but okay. Goodnight!"

In Los Angeles, Peter, the travel photographer, holds his son, Forest, in warm light. Forest seems unusually serious—very, very serious for an otherwise jolly baby. He turns toward the morning sun as Peter, holding him, faces the same direction. With the same stoic expressions and pursed lips, they are biological imprints of each other. Peter manages to capture this moment in a photograph and posts it on Instagram.

"Forest at 9 months 2 days / Me at 39 years 2 days," reads the caption.

After the photographer returned from Norway, he and his girlfriend, Celia, married, and their son arrived on time, eight months after the cruise.

Peter and I exchange emails that are friendly, just personal enough to admit our professional anxieties about the dwindling magazine work but never deep enough to betray our truest fears or wants. Instead, like the rest of the world, I learn of Peter's life-changing milestones and heartfelt sentiments on Instagram.

No, we didn't become Hollywood-style best buds just because we weathered the storm together. For one long day I happened to be his temporary confidant, then we went our separate ways. But I won't forget that, out of the eight billion people on earth, I was among the first to know of his son. I may never get to meet Forest, but I want to see him grow. (There's a Korean saying that it's a destined connection even if your sleeve merely grazes another person's.) So I return to Peter's profile over and over and over.

Inge Lockert responds "No comment" when I message him. He was one of the two local coastal pilots on the ship. It's also a "No comment" from the master of the *Viking Sky*, Captain Bengt-Owe Gustafsson.

Tugboat operator Leif Arne Sørenes takes a long drag of smoke in his living room in Mosterhamn, on the west coast of Norway. "I couldn't sleep that night," he says. "I kept thinking about what could have gone wrong, what I could have done better."

After tugging the *Viking Sky* to safety, the *Vivax*'s crew of four quietly sailed another hour south to Aukra, where the *Vivax* had her base. There was no cheering crowd, no cameramen. In all, he had been up for thirty-eight hours straight, yet he found himself sleepless.

"Seventy-five knots of wind. That is not normal. Eighteen-, twenty-meter swells. That is not normal. Going right up to the aft of the ship to hand over the tug line. That is not normal," he tells me over video chat. "But what can you do?"

This is not just a question of resignation. It's also a question of purpose. What could he and his crew do but help?

Life returned to normal after the incident. Sørenes spends half of each year on the tugboat with Svein Magne, Kenneth, and Bjarne Frank, his family away from family. Even when they're not tugging disabled tankers and assisting container ships, the crew of four have plenty to keep them busy, painting the deck, maintaining the machinery, and, during their free time, fishing for mackerel and herring in the fjords. After all these years, the beauty of the water still astonishes him—each sunrise is a surprise.

The *Viking Sky* is always in the back of his mind, he says. But he and his crew have never spoken of that night.

"It was a hell of a night. We try to forget it. What can you do?" he asks.

From Kerala, India, a man named Kannan calls me on Instagram while steering a car with his free hand. I don't recall ever seeing him before.

"Sir, I know you!" he says. "You were having food from the pool grill. A burger, yes?"

"Wow, you remember!" I say.

"Once I see somebody, I will never forget," he says, proud.

I play along. He probably says this to all the cruise guests. It's a safe bet that every passenger ends up scarfing down a burger by the pool at one point or another.

Right after disembarking, I searched for posts tagged with the *Viking Sky* as their location. Most were by passengers, who interested me little; I'd spent too much time with them already. Besides, they were the only people television stations and newspapers were interviewing. I wanted to hear from the crew. I began following any workers I could find on social media, including Kannan. But if the crew members were traumatized by the events, they didn't show it. In fact, the scant few who mentioned the accident at all quickly deleted those posts. All that's left are filtered images of glamorous globetrotting and triumphant homecoming.

After Hustadvika, Kannan continued working until the pandemic grounded all cruises. Now stuck at home in India, he's feeling the itch to go abroad somewhere, anywhere.

"There was a friendly Indian waiter named Kurien," I say. "He was popular with the old ladies. I know it's a long shot, but do you know who I'm talking about?"

"There are many Indian waiters on the ship," he says.

How stupid of me to message him in the first place, and to ask him about someone just because they both come from the same country, one with a population of 1.3 billion. Still, I grasp at what I can. Kannan did call me in response to my message, after all, unprompted and past midnight my time.

"And how are things in your country?" he asks. "Are there jobs? Is there any chance for me?"

Meanwhile the ship's masseur is trying his luck opening a holistic healing center in a small city in Macedonia. His social media posts are a collage of body parts: his hand rubbing an anonymous hairy thigh; fingers pressing onto a liver-spotted arm; a severed head of Buddha on a New Age-y shrine.

The Serbian aesthetician continues to post glamor shots of her flawless skin, and never twice in the same outfit.

The pastry chef who's been chronicling her fitness journey finally hits her goal weight.

A backup singer opens a sushi takeout stand in Manila.

Another crew member responds to me: "If I share my story with u, do i make some money out of it? I have a small house and the roofing needs complete repair and mom's denture affects her gums. im looking at $1200 to $1700 . . ."

So, all of us, weather-beaten but seaworthy, ride the currents and roll with the waves; we skirt disasters, graze rock bottoms, sail some more. Some of us wash ashore, wrecked; others find refuge in serene coves, ready to drop anchor.

~

Ceri, the Welsh cabaret singer with the patience of a kindergarten teacher, is the only one who hasn't scrubbed her Instagram about the accident. "Update for family & friends: Doing all we can aboard to stay calm and positive. The amazing guests with me in the Atrium are rallying around like family. We are in this together all looking after one another. Humanity really can be ♥#VikingSky.

This is her last post. She never updates her

Instagram after March 23, 2019. Her casting agent lists no more stage credits. Though I can easily find ways to reach her, something tells me she has no desire to rehash events of that night.

I'm relieved to learn the fate of the capsized *Hagland Captain* freighter crew: Helicopter rescuers managed to pluck those nine good Samaritans from the angry sea. The shipping company assures me that they are safe and happily employed. But it won't release their names. I will never know them, these men who almost died while trying to save the cruise passengers.

And what of the men I stepped over while they lay huddled together in the hallway? No matter how I try, they're not to be found using hashtags or location markers on social media. As on the ship, they continue disappearing into thin air.

I can't find the Tagalog-speaking seamen trying to unleash lifeboats in the grainy cell phone footage, either. *Pasok, pasok, pasok*—"Inside, inside, inside" —are the last words I have of them. No names. Just hands and voices floating on the internet.

⁓

The day after we docked in Molde, most of the passengers ended up in the town's small airport. In the waiting area of the three-gate departure hall, the sole kiosk was doing brisk business selling strong coffee and homemade *svele*, a pancake of egg and kefir, folded with *brunost*—which unappetizingly means, in Norwegian, brown cheese. Those who had stayed on the ship swapped stories with those who'd been helicoptered off. And the ones who'd been put up overnight on land compared amenities of their hotels, dissecting the floral bed skirts and wood saunas like giving Tripadvisor reviews.

"Wasn't it just so much fun?" shouted Mary, the roadrunner of a human in her late fifties, when she bumped into me. She was either oblivious of the other passengers' glares—or basking in them. "Oh, I loved it! I wish I could do it again!"

At last, she found a way to enjoy being part of the group.

"I tell you, you couldn't pay for this kind of adventure!" she kept going, breathless. "I loved every minute of that helicopter ride!"

But as she turned away, I saw the corner of her eye twitch just so. Tired? Or, despite what she wants the world to think, was she shaken?

The chorus of passengers kept growing louder and more discordant. I eavesdropped until my flight's final boarding announcement:

"We were standing in that stairway for hours to go up . . ."

"I was just a sack of mail. I was tossed into the helicopter . . ."

"I was so cold, and a volunteer lent me her own coat and hugged me . . ."

"I saw that couple, my god, she broke my heart, she was crying, and they had to pry her hands off her husband. Oh, you've seen him, he has Alzheimer's, you know . . ."

The Prime Minister of Norway, Erna Solberg, tweeted: "It has been a dramatic day for passengers and crew on #VikingSky in #Hustadvika. Thank you to the skilled rescuers, volunteers & others who made an invaluable effort in demanding conditions." She was immediately trolled by the usual Twitter crowd, including a conspiracy theorist who blamed a cabal of Norwegian elites who were sitting on the weather-controlling technology that could have prevented the storm.

On one of the cruise enthusiast message boards, BabyBoomerLass and CruiseGal917 seemed to have made an uneasy truce. But others picked up the virtual vendetta and continued squabbling over what *must* have gone wrong on our cruise.

I don't care about the commenters or conspiracy theorists at the moment; I'm not even thinking about how or why the engines failed. What I want to know is: Whatever happened to housekeeper Ida's tiny Hello Kitty ankle socks? Did that passenger try to send them back? Did they end up in a landfill? Or are they on the passenger's mantel somewhere, a reminder of kindness?

After returning to San Francisco, I set aside my passport and give the whole corporate thing a try. I join a tech company, one of the many, many Silicon Valley firms that equate edginess with misspellings and refusal to use capital letters—so qürky! The start-up says it's "revolutionizing cities." My dad calls it "a taxi company that can't afford its own cars." I don't last long.

It takes me most of a year, but I leave Hannes. There's no final straw. On a beautiful, unremarkable Sunday morning, I sit on the kitchen floor as he slices bread.

"I think it's time I moved out," I say. "I already made arrangements with Jacques last week."

Hannes sits next to me on the floor and holds my hand.

The tearful goodbye stretches across days, weeks, months. Finally, it's the pandemic that draws a hard line. I move out of Jacques's place into my own apartment on the very day the lockdown order begins in San Francisco. As the novel virus confines us inside, I go for days in my spartan, furniture-less studio without seeing another human. I have no salt or sugar; the white walls stay bare for months. But when I think of the life I left behind, I feel more thankful than bereft—thankful to disembark that sinking ship of a relationship, thankful to plant my feet on the firm land of my own choosing.

I recognize, at long last, that the nagging sensation smoldering around my heart has been fury waiting to flare up. I'm so angry, in fact, that I can't bear to write the parts of this book about Hannes until the very last minute. In the end, I write about him only by changing his name and treating him like a character from one of my unfinished novels: someone I've loved and tried to understand and, eventually, will let go.

Those twenty-seven uncertain hours on the cruise were good training ground for what was to come. Now, stuck at home for months in a crowded city, I think of those remote farmhouses I saw from the ship's deck while sailing by with hundreds of people, and I realize I have the kind of life I wanted all along: alone, in the company of others.

For months after arriving home in San Francisco, the memory of the cruise filled me with dread, then bitterness, then sadness; now it also cracks me up. The part I remember the most isn't when we lost power or when the water began flowing in. I think now about the night we spent docked in Molde, where, after the hot shower in the stranger's house, I made my way back to the ship.

Picture this. Waiters have shined their shoes and put on their vests again. They're scurrying around with hamburgers and wine on trays. The PA system comes back on and the captain asks everyone to gather one last time. In spite of being scrubbed and spritzed, the Star Theater still carries a whiff of the hundreds of evacuees who spent the night there. As we file in, I look around and feel a wave swell inside my heart. My story is but one of many here. We will all go our separate ways and tell very different tales. Some of us will dig our heels deeper and become more of who we used to be; some of us will be forever changed by our long night at sea.

Ceri is unrecognizable on stage with her hair slicked back and flipped. After the sleepless night, she's traded in her sensible trousers and parka for a sixties-style mod dress and synthetic knee-highs. She hams it up with the male singers and harmonizes with the other female vocalist, whom I'm still not ready to forgive for that funereal dirge last night—"Hallelujah," my ass. Now, they twirl, clap on stage, and sing, insistently, "Here Comes the Sun."

But wait! Before all that campy insistence on sunshiny days ahead, Viking's CEO makes a surprise appearance. Like a celebrity wrestler, he swaggers down the aisle to thunderous applause; he reaches out and touches passengers' outstretched hands.

Torstein Hagen, who owns three quarters of this seventy-some-vessel company, looks very much like the kind of person who'd take one of his cruises: a snow-haired baby boomer in a casual blazer. He commands the stage with the bonhomie of the father of the bride who's footing the bill, welcoming while making you feel a little indebted to him at the same time.

"I hear the helicopter ride was pretty scary. You're smart to stay on board," he jokes, and the audience guffaws as if this is the most hilarious thing they've ever heard.

Did we have a choice? I sigh and smile. I smile

for all the bad jokes I'll get to hear and tell because I'm alive.

The CEO praises the crew for their attitude and pats himself on the back for having attracted the best kind of customers. He's good. There's a reason why this smooth talker is the CEO.

"What the rescue services did," he continues, "what they've done makes me proud to be Norwegian."

As a closing remark, the CEO adds, almost as an afterthought, that this sailing will be comped for everyone. He has to speak up because the audience grows so loudly approving.

"When you arrive home, you will get an invitation to another Viking cruise," he says, "on my dime."

Everyone's on their feet now, hollering. I will probably never see any of these people again, but together—simply by having sailed on the same ship—they have changed my life. I stand, too. I clap at first just to keep from standing out. The swelling applause drowns my aloofness, and now I'm honestly cheering. I'm cheering for my grandfather's decision to barter his wristwatch, for the editor's pick to commission me a northern lights story, and for every turn and twist in between that led me to this musty auditorium on a cruise ship. Cheering for all the choices I'll get to make.

The CEO shouts over the crowd about how we're free to go anywhere his company travels to. There's no way in hell I'm setting my foot on another cruise ship. But if I can choose, if I really am free to go wherever and do anything, with anyone or on my own, what will I do?

The woman next to me breaks down in joyful tears, her hands cupping her grinning face.

"Can you believe it?" she asks me. "Can you just believe it?"

NOTES

13   *300-year-old Dutch merchant vessel once loaded with*
      yellow bricks: The Stoplelei Wreck and the Dutch Period, an
      exhibit at the University Museum of the Norwegian
      University of Science and Technology. www.ntnu.edu/
      museum/the-stopelei-wreck-and-the-dutch-period

13   *Even experienced fishermen run aground here*: on
      Shipwreck Log, A Log of Shipwrecks & Maritime Accidents
      Around the World. www.shipwrecklog.com/log/tag/
      hustadvika

13   *"strong winds from SW to NW raise a large steep swell with*
      hollow breaking seas": Nautical Publication 57B, *The*
      Admiralty Sailing Directions

18   *the Viking Sky, issued Mayday at two in the afternoon*
      local time on March 23, 2019: Norwegian Rescue
      Services (@HRSSorNorge). Twitter post. March
      23, 2019, 03:08 p.m. twitter.com/HRSSorNorge/
      status/1109456126125490176

18   *Three years ago, the cruise ship took to the water for the first time*: Wepner, Pascal: "*Viking Sky* ist aufgeschwommen auf Fincantieri Werft." March 23, 2016. www.schiffe-und-kreuzfahrten.de/news/viking-sky-ist-aufgeschwommen-auf-fincantieri-werft/89971

18   *about a fifth the size of the largest cruise ship in service*:

"Symphony of the Seas." Royal Caribbean. www.royalcaribbean.com/cruise-ships/ symphony-of-the-seas

"*Viking Sky*." Fincateri. www.fincantieri.com/en/ products-and-services/cruise-ships/viking-sky

19   *sixty-foot waves and eighty-seven-mile-per-hour winds*: Cappucci, Matthew. "A Cruise Ship Sailed into an Intense Cyclone. These Warning Signs Showed Trouble Was Brewing at Sea." *Washington Post*, March 25, 2019. www.washingtonpost.com/ weather/2019/03/25/cruise-ship-sailed-into-an-intense-cyclone-these-warning-signs-showed-trouble-was-brewing-sea/

19   *canceled all regional ferries*: Hagen, Angelica. "Bengt-Owe Gustafsson styrte «Viking Sky»: - Gjorde sitt beste." *Dagbladet*. March 26, 2019. www.dagbladet. no/nyheter/bengt-owe-gustafsson-styrte-viking-sky---gjorde-sitt-beste/70912342

25   *They can't spend more than a few seconds pushing each passenger into the tender*: Spinks, Rosie. "What the *Viking Sky* Cruise Evacuation Tells Us About Cruise Ship Safety." *Quartz*, March 25, 2019. qz.com/quartzy/1579782/is-cruising-safe-what-the-viking-sky-cruise-evacuation-tells-us

26   *This is where the footage ends*: "VIDEO: Kaadrid Norras merehätta sattunud laevalt (NB! Nõrganärvilistele

mittesoovitav!)" *Eestinen.* March 23, 2019.
eestinen.fi/2019/03/video-kaadrid-norras-merehatta-
sattunud-laevalt-nb-norganarvilistele-mittesoovitav

26   *the ship was a mere eleven miles south of Old Head
of Kinsale*: "#Lusitania Centennial #OnThisday:
#Lusitania100 years #LusitaniaRemembered #Cobh
#Kinsale #Lusitania100Cork #Cork" The Lusitania
Resource *History, Passenger & Crew Biographies, and
Lusitania Facts.* May 8, 2015. www.rmslusitania.info/
lusitania-centennial-onthisday-lusitania100-years-
lusitaniaremembered-cobh-kinsale-lusitania100cork-
cork

26   *dumping the passengers into the sea*:

      Preston, Diana. "Torpedoed!" *Smithsonian
Magazine.* May 2002. www.smithsonianmag.com/
history/torpedoed-62260018

      Sides, Anna Goodwin. "New Clues in *Lusitania*'s
Sinking." *NPR.* November 22, 2008. www.npr.org/
templates/story/story.php?storyId=97350149

27   *1,198 lives were lost*: Encyclopaedia Britannica, s.v.
"*Lusitania*, British Ship." www.britannica.com/topic/
Lusitania-British-ship

27   *killed 862 crewmen*: "Sinking." *The HMS* Barham
Association. www.hmsbarham.com/ship/sinking.php

27   *cameraman John Turner filmed the scene*: McKernan,
Luke. "John Turner." The *Guardian,* March 24,
2007. www.theguardian.com/news/2007/mar/24/
guardianobituaries.obituaries

28   *five million views and counting! More than 18,000 "likes"*:
British Pathé, "HMS *Barham* Explodes & Sinks: World
War II (1941) | British Pathé" YouTube video, July 27,
2011. www.youtube.com/watch?v=YdrISbwy_zI

30   *Captain Francesco Schettino steered off its planned course*: Squires, Nick. "*Costa Concordia* Trial: I Was Captain's Lover, Admits Moldovan Dancer." The *Telegraph*, October 29, 2013. www.telegraph.co.uk/news/worldnews/europe/italy/10412663/Costa-Concordia-trial-I-was-captains-lover-admits-Moldovan-dancer.html

30   *Today, he's still serving time in prison*: "*Costa Concordia* Captain's Sentence Upheld by Italy Court." BBC, May 12, 2017. www.bbc.com/news/world-europe-39903968

30   *neither of which is catching*: Nilsen, Sondre, and Ingvild Silseth: "lik var det dramatiske døgnet for *Viking Sky*" *VG*, accessed in 2020. www.vg.no/spesial/2019/viking-sky-evakuering/

35   *Sailing now is foolish*: Leif Arne Sørenes, in conversation with the author, August 2020.

35   *more than eighty-six miles per hour*: Cappucci, Matthew. "A Cruise Ship Sailed into an Intense Cyclone. These Warning Signs Showed Trouble Was Brewing at Sea." *Washington Post*, March 25, 2019. www.washingtonpost.com/weather/2019/03/25/cruise-ship-sailed-into-an-intense-cyclone-these-warning-signs-showed-trouble-was-brewing-sea/

36   *a little over a hundred feet*: "*Vivax*." Østensjø — Fleet. ostensjo.no/fleet/vivax

36   *built to pull tankers and cruise ships*: Ekker, Bjørn. 2019. "Kapteinen På Slepebåten «Vivax»: – Vi Hadde Ikke Gjort Det Om vi Ikke Var Helt Nødt." *VG*. March 25, 2019. www.vg.no/nyheter/innenriks/i/awlb85/kapteinen-paa-slepebaaten-vivax-vi-hadde-ikke-gjort-det-om-vi-ikke-var-helt-noedt

36   *have since given up on assisting and left*: Vessel Tracker. 2019. "Cruise Ship 'Viking Sky' Suffered from Engine

Failure | March 23, 2019." YouTube.
www.youtube.com/watch?v=gy7J8JvIcjw

36   *Norwegian law requires local coastal pilots*: Walker, Jim.
"Independence of the Seas Arrested in Norway." *Cruise
Law News.* May 22, 2014. www.cruiselawnews
.com/2014/05/articles/worst-cruise-line-in-the-world/
independence-of-the-seas-arrested-in-norway/

39   *he hopes to be there to help*: Jim H. Nielsen, in
conversation with the author, June 2020.

43   *low pressure swirling between Iceland and Norway*:
Cappucci, Matthew. 2019. "A Cruise Ship Sailed
into an Intense Cyclone. These Warning Signs
Showed Trouble Was Brewing at Sea." *Washington
Post*, March 25, 2019. www.washingtonpost.com/
weather/2019/03/25/cruise-ship-sailed-into-an-
intense-cyclone-these-warning-signs-showed-trouble-
was-brewing-sea

45   *Joseph Conrad ripped into the tabloid*: Conrad, Joseph.
(1912) 2012. "Some Reflections on the Loss of
the *Titanic*," *Notes on Life and Letters.* eBook. Start
Publishing

50   *It takes awhile before he lands*: Erlend Birkeland, in
conversation with the author, July 2020.

51   *their robes flapping like a superhero's cape*: Oliver, David.
2019. "Five Helicopters, 28 Rescuers, 464 Saved:
Inside the *Viking Sky* Cruise Ship Rescue." *USA Today.*
March 28, 2019. www.usatoday.com/story/travel/
cruises/2019/03/28/viking-sky-cruise-ship-norway-
inside-rescue-mission/3298517002/

54   *we'd come close to capsizing*: Mauren, Arnfinn,
Robert Veiåker Johansen, Marthe Øvergård, and
Christian Sørgjerd. 2019. "Jubel og tårer ved
cruise-marerittets slutt." *Aftenposten.* March 24,

2019. www.aftenposten.no/norge/i/g7w6z5/
Jubel-og-tarer-ved-cruise-marerittets-slutt

54 *Norway's most widely read daily newspaper*: "Opplagstall Norske Aviser." Medienorge. www.medienorge.uib.no/ statistikk/medium/avis/190

54 *as close as sixteen inches from meeting the underwater rocks*: Hattrem, Hanne, Amalie Frøystad Nærø, Benedicte Bratås, Signe Rosenlund-hauglid, Andrea Rognstrand, and Jørgen Braastad. 2019. "«Viking Sky»: Kan Ha Vært 40 Centimeter Fra Bunnen." *VG*. March 29, 2019. www.vg.no/nyheter/innenriks/i/1n6y2X/ viking-sky-kan-ha-vaert-40-centimeter-fra-bunnen

54 *grinding against the ten-foot-shallow seabed*: Roaldseth, Sara Lovise, Julie Vissgren, Jøte Toftaker, Einar Orten Trovåg. *NRK*. March 24, 2019. www.nrk.no/mr/_- skipet-har-vaert-skrekkelig-langt-inne-1.14487736

57 *some ports even force the bulky vessels to leave when a hurricane approaches*: "A Ship in the Storm — Interview with Captain Henri Scheer." 2017. Hapag-Lloyd. October 20, 2017. www.hapag-lloyd.com/en/news- insights/insights/2017/10/interview-of-the-week.html

57 *the 100-yard-long cargo ship changed course*: "Hagland Captain." vesseltracker.com. www.vesseltracker.com/ en/Ships/Hagland-Captain-9521356.html

58 *"is bound to proceed with all speed to their assistance"*: "Chapter V — Regulation 33 — Distress Situations: Obligations and Procedures." 2019. SOLAS Convention, 1974. solasv.mcga.gov.uk/regulations/ regulation33.htm

59 *tries to fight the maelstrom, its engines stall*: "Lasteskipet Hagland Captain." 2019. NRK. March 27, 2019. www.nrk.no/mr/lasteskipet-hagland-captain-1.14489350

59 *At 4,599 tons of deadweight*: "Hagland Captain." 2013. *Hagland.* www.hagland.com/fleet/hagland-captain

59 *"We are capsizing"*: Nielsen, Jim H., and David Abad. 2019. "What Went Right! The *Viking Sky* Rescue Mission through the Eyes of the Crew." *InterPilot: The Journal of the International Federation of Airline Pilots' Association.* 2019 vol. 3, 20 – 25. www.ifalpa.org

59 *a mix of his native Danish and his colleagues' Norwegian*: Jim H. Nielsen, in conversation with the author, June 2020.

61 *long enough for a rescuer to fish them out*:

   "Lasteskipet *Hagland Captain*." *NRK.* March 27, 2019. www.nrk.no/mr/ lasteskipet-hagland-captain-1.14489350

   Frøystad Nærø, Amalie, and Jørgen Braastad. 2019. "Mannskapet Måtte Hoppe På Sjøen: – Det Var Alvorlig." *VG.* March 26, 2019. www.vg.no/ nyheter/innenriks/i/jdQQdw/mannskapet-maatte-hoppe-paa-sjoeen-det-var-alvorlig

79 *the result of the sun spitting electrons and protons*: "What Causes the Northern Lights?" *NASA Goddard Space Flight Center.* pwg.gsfc.nasa.gov/polar/telecons/ archive/PR_E-PO/Aurora_flyer

79 *bright spectacles near the magnetic poles*: "What Are the Northern Lights?" 2015. *Everyday Mysteries.* The Library of Congress. 2015. www.loc.gov/everyday-mysteries/item/ what-are-the-northern-lights/

80 *red fox, dragons, whale's plumes, the coming of the French Revolution, and spirits fighting while being egged on by humans*:

"Dark Side of the Auroras — Meanings and Myths," *Visit Finnish Lapland*. October 31, 2017. www.lapland.fi/visit/only-in-lapland/lapland-northern-lights-myths-auroras/

"Mythology of the Northern Lights." *The Aurora Zone*. 2014. www.theaurorazone.com/about-the-aurora/aurora-legends

80   *the dead trying to speak to you*: Karen Nyheim, in conversation with the author, March 2020

84   *gale force enough to veer a car on the road*: "Wind Speed Units & Wind Directions Converter." *Windfinder*. www.windfinder.com/wind/windspeed.htm

91   *"a strange sort of insanity came over me"*: Herman Melville, *Moby-Dick; or, The Whale*. New York: Harper & Brothers, 1851. Chapter 94. mel-juxta-editions.herokuapp.com/documents/451

92   *"higher horror" of whitewashed ruins in Lima*: Ibid. Chapter 42. mel-juxta-editions.herokuapp.com/documents/399

92   *"all-color of atheism from which we shrink?"*: Ibid. Chapter 42. mel-juxta-editions.herokuapp.com/documents/399

93   *"giving the white man ideal mastership over every dusky tribe"*: Herman Melville, *Moby-Dick; or, The Whale*. New York: Harper & Brothers, 1851. Chapter 42. mel-juxta-editions.herokuapp.com/documents/399

95   *who were none too happy about their intrusion*: Linden, Eugene. "The Vikings: A Memorable Visit to America." *Smithsonian*, December 2004. www.smithsonianmag.com/history/the-vikings-a-memorable-visit-to-america-98090935/

96   *the preferred mode of crossing the Atlantic in the mid-twentieth century*: Stevenson, Seth. "How Did the Cruise Industry Become Synonymous With Disaster?" *Slate.* May 22, 2020. slate.com/business/2020/05/cruise-industry-disaster-history-coronavirus.html

96   *the ship turned into a veritable vomitorium*: Mayerowitz, Scott. "400-Plus Passengers Get Sick on Cruise." *ABC News.* February 23, 2010. abcnews.go.com/Travel/vomiting-diarrhea-hit-celebrity-mercury-learn-stay-healthy/story?id=9920566

96   *float aimlessly without plumbing*: Griffin, Drew, and Scott Bronstein, "'Poop Cruise' Carnival Triumph Set Sail with Problems." CNN. December 18, 2013. www.cnn.com/2013/12/17/travel/carnival-cruise-triumph-problems/index.html

96   *quietly changed the ship's name to the less triumphant* Sunrise: Tribou, Richard. "Old Ship, New Name: Carnival *Sunrise* Debuts in Fort Lauderdale." *Orlando Sentinel.* October 29, 2019. www.orlandosentinel.com/travel/florida-cruise-guide/os-tr-cru-carnival-sunrise-fort-lauderdale-debut-20191029-vbsq2mhqang3dbcdpufbppk4le-story.html

97   *connects the word to* tripalium, *an ancient Roman method of torture*: "Definition of travail." Merriam-Webster.com. www.merriam-webster.com/dictionary/travail

101   *help me decipher love in the time of PrEP*: I shamelessly stole this from the title of my friend Jacques Rancourt's beautiful poetry collection, *In the Time of PrEP*, published by the *Beloit Poetry Journal.*

105   *2.4 million ethnic Koreans living in Japan*: 윤인진. "코리안 디아스포라의 역사." 코리안 디아스포라 국제 학술 컨퍼런스. ggc.ggcf.kr/p/5cbef73a3c56f44ce491bc92

105 *its famous traditional troupe of male-impersonating actresses*: Takarazuka Revue. kageki.hankyu.co.jp

106 *acting on intelligence that there were 2,000 Japanese soldiers on board*: "'곤론마루 폭침' 추모제에 한국 유족 첫 참가." 2013. KBS News. October 3, 2013. news.kbs.co.kr/news/view.do?ncd=2733106

106 *a derailed train had stranded those soldiers on land in Japan*: 김민주. 2016. "오인 격침당한 `곤론마루호` 희생자 부산서 73년 만에 추도식." 국제신문. October 5, 2016. www.kookje.co.kr/news2011/asp/newsbody.asp?code=0300&key=20161006.22006194642

106 *More than 580 would perish*: 김상진. 2014. "곤론마루 호의 비극을 아십니까?" 부산경남대표방송. October 3, 2014. www.knn.co.kr/35957

106 *On board were more than 4,000 Koreans*: 고병준. 2020. "N. Korea Demands Japan's Apology over Killing of Korean Forced Workers in 'Ukishima Maru Sinking.'" *Yonhap News Agency*. August 24, 2020. en.yna.co.kr/view/AEN20200824001700325

106 *the ship struck a magnetic mine*: 민소영. "조선인 귀국선 '우키시마마루' 폭침 74주기… 일본 각지서 추모 행사." 부산일보. August 25, 2019. www.busan.com/view/busan/view.php?code=20190825184309933305.

106 *More than 500 passengers drowned*: "*Ukishima Maru* Victims Lost Redress in '50." The *Japan Times*. September 28, 2003. www.japantimes.co.jp/news/2003/09/28/national/ukishima-maru-victims-lost-redress-in-50/

107 *some scholars and the victims' descendants believe the explosion was no accident*: 김문길. "우키시마 폭침사건에 관한 연구." 성찰과 전망. Vol. 22, October 2016. blog.daum.net/meezou/162

108 *Japanese government banned the native language in schools in Korea*: 허동현 "'일본어만 쓰고 말하라'. . . 일제의 한국어 말살정책 본격화." 중앙일보. March 17, 2010. news.joins.com/article/4063980

110 *Fifteen hours*: Leif Arne Sørenes, in conversation with the author, August 2020.

117 *a common genetic mutation that my people carry*: Engelhaupt, Erika. "What Your Earwax Says about Your Ancestry." *Science News*. February 25, 2014. www.sciencenews.org/blog/gory-details/ what-your-earwax-says-about-your-ancestry

123 *From the outside, the ship looks absolutely normal*: "Norway Cruise Ship Arrives at Port after Passenger Airlifts." *BBC*, March 24, 2019. www.bbc.com/news/ world-europe-47685595

128 *identified low lubricating oil as the reason for the debacle*: Norwegian Safety Investigation Authority. "Investigation of Marine Accident at Hustadvika, Møre Og Romsdal County." *Havarikommisjonen*. November 12, 2019. havarikommisjonen.no/Sjofart/ Undersokelser/19-2621

128 *the sloshing oil failed to reach the pumps*:

Thompson, Julia. "*Viking Sky* Cruise Ship Engines Failed Because of Low Oil Levels, Maritime Official Says." *USA Today*, March 27, 2019. www.usatoday.com/story/travel/cruises/ 2019/03/27/viking-sky-cruise-ship-engines- failed-lack-oil-official-says/3288348002/

Arnfinn Mauren and Wasim Riaz: "Viking Sky-blackout'en: Lavt oljetrykk var årsaken." *Aftenposten*, March 27, 2019. www.aftenposten.no/norge/i/8mpl8Q/ viking-sky-blackouten-lavt-oljetrykk-var-aarsaken

128 *the engines automatically shut down*: "NMA: *Viking Sky* Engine Failure Caused by Low Oil Pressure." *Maritime Executive*. www.maritime-executive.com/article/nma-viking-sky-engine-failure-caused-by-low-oil-pressure

129 *In Aalborg, Denmark*: Jim H. Nielsen, in conversation with the author, June 2020.

130 *puts his hands behind his head and leans back*: Erlend Birkeland, in conversation with the author, July 2020.

130 *dropped halfway between Scotland and Norway*: Ellers, Fred S. 1982. "Advanced Offshore Oil Platforms." *Scientific American* 246 (4): 38–49.

131 *Forest at 9 months 2 days / Me at 39 years 2 days*: Bohler, Peter. @PeterBohler. Instagram post. www.instagram.com/peterbohler/

132 *"I couldn't sleep that night"*: Leif Arne Sørenes, in conversation with the author, August 2020.

133 *"Sir, I know you!"* Except for the captain and the local pilot, all *Viking Sky* crew members' names were changed to ensure their anonymity.

138 *"made an invaluable effort in demanding conditions"*: Solberg, Erna. Twitter post, March 24, 2019. twitter.com/erna_solberg/status/1109792143936311296

141 *who owns three quarters of this seventy-some-vessel company*: Debter, Lauren. "Viking Saga: The Tale of Tor Hagen And His Voyage From Ousted CEO To Cancer Survivor To Cruise Ship Billionaire." *Forbes*, April 15, 2019. www.forbes.com/sites/laurendebter/2019/04/15/meet-the-man-who-started-viking-cruises-in-his-50s-after-being-fired-losing-millions-and-surviving-cancer

Throughout the book, I cross-referenced articles from various sources ranging from the Norwegian newspapers *Aftenposten, Dagbladet,* and *VG* to English-language broadcasters such as BBC, CNN, and ABC, as well as news coverage by the Norwegian public broadcasting company NRK.

I relied most heavily on Aftenposten's complete coverage (www.aftenposten.no/emne/viking-sky) and the interactive feature by Sondre Nilsen and Ingvild Silseth at *VG* (www.vg.no/spesial/2019/viking-sky-evakuering).

Facts about the *Viking Sky*, such as its dimensions and weight, are from the manufacturer Fincantieri's website: www.fincantieri.com/en/products-and-services/cruise-ships/viking-sky.

If you have a hard time falling asleep at night and can't get into *Moby-Dick*, *VG* has more than fifteen hours of live TV coverage still available online for free: www.vgtv.no/video/173685/se-seningen-slepingen-av-cruiseskipet-viking-sky.

ABC put together a montage of social-media clips of the incident, available at: www.abc7chicago.com/hustadvika-viking-sky-stranded-cruise-ship-norway/5215926.

The primary source for this book, however, is the notes I scribbled on my phone during the twenty-seven hours at sea.

ACKNOWLEDGMENTS

Thank you for—

   your selflessness: the crew, rescue workers, and
   volunteers who assisted the *Viking Sky*, especially Erlend
   Birkeland, Jim H. Nielsen, Leif Arne Sørenes;

   your faith: Joshua Bodwell and the entire Godine family;

   the journey: Michael Lowenthal;

   the light and shade: Jacques Rancourt, Julie Yeagle;

   the beacon: the teachers I've been privileged to have,
   too many to name all;

   the fellowship: writers—especially Hilary Zaid, Jamel
   Brinkley, Jaquira Diaz, Jessamine Chan, Karin Davidson,
   Leland Cheuk, Michelle Peñaloza, Sarah Cypher;

   the rescue line: Faith and Travis Hall;

   the sustenance: Amanda Doster, Alex Riechel, Cheryl
   Chang, Jenjira Yahirun, Uju Anya, Walter Cheng;

   the clarity: Brian Francisco, Megan McCrea, Sveinung
   Zahl, Thor Carey, Trevor Cox;

   the years of support: Laura Cogan and Oscar Villalon at
   Zyzzyva, and the Bread Loaf Writers' Conference;

   the generosity: the Brown Handler Writers' Residency,
   the Friends of the San Francisco Public Library,
   Caldera, Key West Literary Seminar, Wildacres, and the
   workshops at the Community of Writers, Napa Valley
   and Tomales Bay.

Most of all, Dad, Mom, Sebin, Serine—every story I tell is
because of you.

ABOUT THE AUTHOR

Chaney Kwak has been traversing the globe for more than a decade to write about food and travel. His work appears regularly in newspapers such as the *New York Times* and the *Wall Street Journal*, as well as magazines such as *Afar, Condé Nast Traveler,* and *Travel + Leisure.* Mr. Kwak teaches nonfiction writing with the Stanford Continuing Studies program and lives in San Francisco.

A NOTE ON THE TYPE

The Passenger has been set in New Baskerville, a contemporary typeface based on the work of John Baskerville (1706–1775), an English printer revered for his masterpiece Folio Bible printed for Cambridge University in 1763. This late-twentieth-century interpretation of Baskerville's style is known for being elegant yet readable.

Book Design by Brooke Koven
Composition by Tammy Ackerman